ANDREW MARTIN

INTERIOR DESIGN REVIEW VOLUME 25

teNeues

1996   '97   '98   '99   2000   '01

Michael Reeves wins the '98 Award

Design Awards launched at the V&A 19th June 1996

Thomas Pheasant is the first US designer to win

Nelson Mandela congratulates South Africas Stephen Falcke on winning the fourth award

Belgiums Jean de Meulder wins

Jo Malone is a judge

Rory Bremnar presents at the V&A Museum

Vol. 1

Kelly Hoppen wins 1st award

Vol. 3

Vol. 4

Alberto Pinto on the cover

Vol. 2

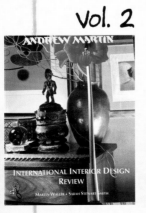

Back cover John Minshaw

Vol. 5

Terry O'Neil & Darcey Bussell join the judging panel

'02   '03   '04   '05   '06   '07   '08

Amanda Rosa is the 6th winner

Jamie Drake becomes the 2nd American winner

Taylor Howes are the 10th winners

2008 Winner Kit Kemp

Zaha Hadid is one of the stars in Volume 12

Turkeys Zeynep Fadillioglu is the first woman in history to design a mosque and wins the 7th award

Vol. 10

ANDREW MARTIN
INTERIOR DESIGN REVIEW
FEATURING THE WORLD'S LEADING DESIGNERS

Tara Bernerd wins

Tara Bernerd

DESIGNER: TARA BERNERD
COMPANY: TARGET LIVING, LONDON, ENGLAND

Projects: Houses and apartments in large luxury residential developments, commercial commissions for spaces such as art galleries. Has just launched her own line of furniture

Norways Helene Hennie wins in Oslo

ANDREW MARTIN
INTERIOR DESIGN REVIEW
FEATURING THE WORLD'S LEADING DESIGNERS

Vol. 12

Anya Hindmarch is a judge

Gabby Logan with Christine Yorath

Celebrities join the party

Tamara Ecclestone

2007 the awards are launched in China

Ben Fogle

ANDREW MARTIN
INTERIOR DESIGN REVIEW

Featuring the World's leading designers

Vol. 6

Marie Helvin

Awards dinner held at the Haymarket Hotel

Twiggy & daughter Carly

Gordon Ramsey, Richard E. Grant, Twiggy & Tim Rice join the judging panel

The Duchess of York is a judge

Darcey Bussell

Tara Palmer-Tomkinson

3

Axel Vervoordt is presented with the 2009 award at his castle in Antwerp

Sharon & Kelly Osborne present Martyn Lawrence-Bullard with the 14th award in Los Angeles

Back in London the award goes to Lebanon's Rabih Hage

The New York Times Square billboard announces the 1st Asian winner, Hong Kong's One Plus Design

Rose Uniacke the 17th award winner

The award moves to Geneva for the presentation to Jorge Canete

Steve Leung wins in Shanghai

ANDREW MARTIN

INTERIOR DESIGN REVIEW

FEATURING THE WORLD'S LEADING DESIGNERS

Vol. 13

Thandiwe Newton is a judge

Japanese designers celebrate at the British Embassy, Tokyo

Vol. 18

Vol. 19

25 Years of the Andrew Martin Awards

'16   '17   '18   '19   '20   2021

Nicky Haslam receives the 20th award at the Design Museum, London

Stephen Fry presents Erin Martin with 2017 award at the Royal Academy, London

Tony Duquettes Dawnridge sees Ohara Davies-Gaetano receive the 22nd award

Duan Curry arrives at the British Embassy in Washington to receive the 2019 award

Awards are back in Shanghai for hometown winner Ben Wu

Ronnie Wood & Kelly Jones are the judges

Vol. 22

Vol. 23

Vol. 24

Thomas Jayne is the winner of the 25th award

Vol. 21

Vol. 20

Kit Kemp & Jade Jagger are judges

Liz Hurley is a judge

Olympic champion Seb Coe judges

Vol. 25

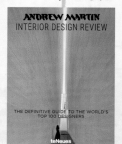

5

For a quarter of a century, I have been lucky enough to have a front row seat at the theatre of the world's greatest designers.

I have called this exhilarating mosaic of styles and influences the Kaleidoscope Age. Since 1996, the Andrew Martin Review has endeavoured to somehow capture the ever-changing refraction of the history, politics and zeitgeist of interior design.

Compare and contrast the work of just a few of the 25 winners of the award; from the groundbreaking East meets West mantra of Kelly Hoppen in 1996, the history making Zeynep Fadillioglu when she became the first woman ever to design a mosque, the supremely influential austerity of Axel Vervoordt, Stephen Falcke the evangelist of African tribal art, the exuberance of Kit Kemp, the celebrity circus of Martyn Lawrence Bullard, the poetic magic of Jorge Cañete and in 2020 the standard bearer of China's golden generation of design, Ben Wu.

The task of selecting a single award winner is always an agonising assignment. Luckily, this year our judges were legendary Rolling Stone Ronnie Wood, iconic Stereophonics front man Kelly Jones, producer actress Sally Humphreys and talent director Jakki Jones.

Astutely, they picked the world renowned designer and scholar Thomas Jayne. He is perhaps the foremost interpreter of historic American interiors. He adds one more layer to the Kaleidoscope.

Martin Waller

JAYNE DESIGN STUDIO

Designer: Thomas Jayne. **Company:** Jayne Design Studio, New York City, USA. Creating personal, comfortable interiors that are grounded in the present and influenced by the past. Unifying ancient and modern for over three decades, the firm is known for inventive details and references to historical decoration. Recent work includes The Directors House at the Winterthur Museum, a seaside cottage in Oyster Bay, and an important 18th century house in Charleston. Current projects include a new house in Pacific Palisades, an early 20th century Spanish cottage in Santa Barbara, the restoration of a Colonial Revival house in Greenwich, a modern apartment overlooking Independence Hall in Philadelphia, and a pre war duplex apartment in Manhattan. **Design philosophy:** tradition is now.

Designer: Kar-Hwa Ho. **Company:** Zaha Hadid Architects, London, UK. Working with clients who have a global reputation for excellence, ZHA has redefined architecture for the 21st century, with a repertoire of projects that have captured imaginations across the globe. Current work includes high end luxury retail in Shanghai, a bespoke residential interior for a townhouse in Hong Kong and corporate headquarters in Guangzhou. Recent projects include hotels in Dubai and Macau and a residential condominium in Miami. **Design philosophy:** optically rich interiors are built essays in spatial composition that invite perception and encourage exploration. These acts of participation instil a sense of personal ownership in visitors as they interact with each other and the surrounding architecture.

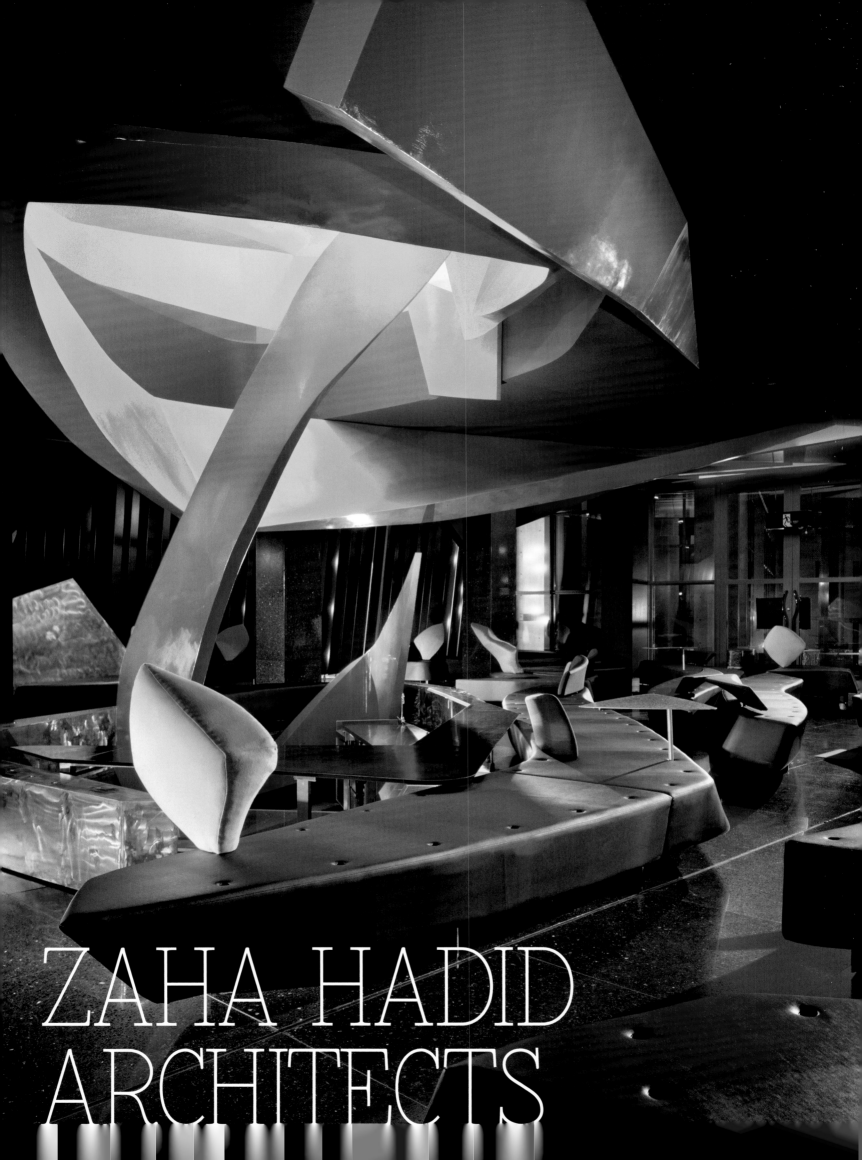

ZAHA HADID
ARCHITECTS

IDMEN LIU

Designers: Idmen Liu. **Company:** Idmatrix, Shenzhen, China. IDMatrix originates from Matrix Design, an academic research centre dedicated to the practical operation of full life cycle design. IDMatrix uses 'New Asia' aesthetics and forms the concept of 'Return to the East' in terms of sustainability, culture, art and philosophy. Currently, IDMatrix focus on urban renewal and future communities, rural construction and 'post urbanization' development, and are committed to the academic restoration of old buildings. **Design philosophy:** sustainability, culture, art, philosophy.

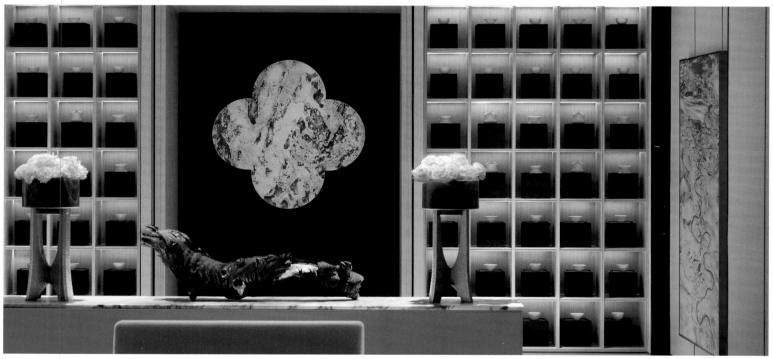

25

KATIE RIDDER

Designer: Katie Ridder. **Company:** Katie Ridder Inc, New York City, USA. Specialising in uniquely imaginative residential interiors in the US, and designer of a signature line of wallpaper and fabrics. Current projects include an oceanfront house in New York, a family house in Dallas, in collaboration with Katie's husband, architect Peter Pennoyer, and apartments on 5th Avenue and Central Park West in New York City. Recent work includes residences in Alabama and California, and the renovation of a 5th Avenue apartment in New York City. **Design philosophy:** exuberantly colorful traditionalism.

ZHANG CAN & LI WENTING

Designers: Zhang Can & Li Wenting. **Company:** CSD Design, Chengdu, China. Specialising in resort hotels, cultural creative space, art galleries and museums. Current projects include a resort hotel in Yaan, a museum hotel in Mianyang, and another resort hotel in Jianmenguan. Recent work includes Xindi boutique hotel in Songyang, Bodu resort hotel in Tengchong, and a visitor centre in Bingling Grottoes. **Design philosophy:** unique spaces, ideological experiences.

GRACINHA VITERBO

Designer: Gracinha Viterbo. **Company:** Viterbo Interior Design, Lisbon, Portugal. Founded 40 years ago, Viterbo is a family owned studio specialising in luxurious interiors for private homes and boutique hotels internationally. Recent projects include a 19th century palace restoration in Lisbon, the décor of the most exclusive building in Lisbon, Castilho 203, and a beautiful estate in Tuscany. Current work includes a 5 star hotel in the Azores, an exclusive beach house in Quinta do Lago, Algarve and another in Comporta. **Design philosophy:** personalised and unique.

ALBION NORD

Designers: Camilla Clarke, Ottalie Stride, Ben Johnson, Anthony Kooperman. **Company:** Albion Nord, London, UK. Interior design studio specialising in high end residential properties and hospitality projects in the UK and overseas. Current residential projects include a private country manor house in Oxfordshire, a family home in Maida Vale and a Landmark Hotel in London. Recent works include a private country estate in Berkshire, two townhouses in Chelsea Barracks and a scheme of 25 apartments in Holland Park. **Design philosophy:** authentic and curated, combining old and new.

ROUGE ABSOLU

Designer: Géraldine B. Prieur. **Company:** ROUGE ABSOLU, Paris, London, Los Angeles. Luxury interior architecture and design in France as well as internationally, for residential, hotels and private jets. The studio also designs scénography for prestigious international brands. Current projects include houses in Paris and in London, a villa in Los Angeles, and a private plane in Dubai. Recent work includes a prestigious villa in the Hamptons, a magical scénography for a French luxury brand, and a residential project in London for a celebrity. **Design philosophy:** create the daring.

OLGA SEDOVA & PROKHOR MASHUKOV

Designers: Olga Sedova & Prokhor Mashukov. **Company:** ONLY design, Moscow, Russia. Specialising in the interiors of apartments and houses in Russia and overseas, as well as cafes and restaurants. Current projects include a house in Luxembourg and a house and apartment in the Moscow region. Recent works include an apartment in Riga, a house in Slovenia and apartments in Moscow. **Design philosophy:** glam punk.

MAIRA KOUTSOUDAKIS

Designer: Maira Koutsoudakis. **Company:** LIFE Interiors, Johannesburg, South Africa. Specialising in exclusive, sustainable design, in 20 countries, for over 20 years. Current work includes listed finca homes, an eco retreat and art galleries in Segera and Arijiju in Kenya; the restoration of a 6 storey Bauhaus heritage home in Tel Aviv; a contemporary penthouse in Lagos and a sprawling villa in the Cradle of Humankind, South Africa. Recent work includes Islas Secas, an eco retreat peninsula of 14 private islands in Panama; North Island, a private development in the Seychelles; a cluster of luxury Greek island homes in Serifos; three desert oases in Namibia, and two eco camps in the jungles of the Congo. **Design philosophy:** island specialists in hospitality, heritage & sustainability, afficionados of contemporary organic chic.

BEN WU

Designer: Ben Wu. **Company:** W.DESIGN, Shanghai, China. Founded by the 2020 designer of the year Ben Wu, W. DESIGN has been developing the philosophy of new life theories based on Chinese traditional culture. The team has constructed a grouping of architecture, interior design, decoration and product design professionals that has achieved strategic co-operations with China's top 50 estate brands. Current projects include show rooms in Tianjin and Shanghai, and a luxury villa in Shanghai. Recent work includes a show room in Shaoxing, and villas in Shanghai. **Design philosophy:** Modern Orientalism.

WOODSON & RUMMERFIELD

Designers: Ron Woodson & Jaime Rummerfield. **Company:** Woodson & Rummerfield's House of Design, L.A. USA. Revered tastemakers specialising in residential and commercial interiors which combine history, heritage and opulence for a discerning clientele. Current projects include a family residence in San Francisco, a Bauhaus beach house restoration in Maine, and a roof top corporate office, art gallery and penthouse in Los Angeles. Recent work includes a historic preservation residence by master architect Richard Neutra in Hollywood, a large family home in Atherton, California, and historic estates in Los Feliz and Beverly Hills, California. **Design philosophy:** modern opulence.

STÉPHANIE COUTAS

Designer: Stéphanie Coutas. **Company**: Stéphanie Coutas, Paris, France. An international team of twenty talented multilingual experts, working in close collaboration with top French artisans and internationally renowned artists. Projects include apartments, pieds-à-terre, penthouses, hotels, spas & restaurants. Current projects include three houses in St.Tropez, where the team are working on both the landscaping and interior renovation, a penthouse in Paris with a 300 sq. m. terrace, and roof garden, and a hotel in the South of France, which is part of a new Art de Vivre chain. Recent work includes a beautiful Art Déco house in Paris, a beach side villa in St Barts, and a new apartment overlooking the Eiffel Tower. **Design philosophy**: blending art de vivre with distinct heritage and culture.

SOPHIE PATERSON

Designer: Sophie Paterson. **Company:** Sophie Paterson Interiors, UK. Specialising in luxury interior design and interior architecture in the UK and overseas including private homes and residential developments. Current projects include two substantial villas in Oman, a large new build house in North London and multiple listed properties across Chelsea, Kensington and Knightsbridge. Recent work includes a Georgian townhouse in Kensington, a new build contemporary penthouse in Mayfair and an apartment in Chelsea barracks. **Design philosophy:** liveable luxury.

Designer: Mary Douglas Drysdale.
Company: Mary Douglas Drysdale Interiors, Washington, USA. An architectural interiors practice with expertise in both historic and modern architecture, decoration and art placement. Current projects include the interior design of a modern house by Dutch architect Piet Boone, developing and designing The Gate House Dupont, a luxury destination for art collectors and designers, and working on the design scheme for the house of a well known Washington artist. Recent work includes a modern penthouse apartment in Boston, a penthouse apartment in Bethesda, Maryland, Design Chair of Aspire House McLean, Virginia, a Park Avenue apartment in New York, and an estate in Pebble Beach, California. **Design philosophy:** the creation of beautiful and highly functional interiors in collaboration with our clients.

MARY

DOUGLAS DRYSDALE

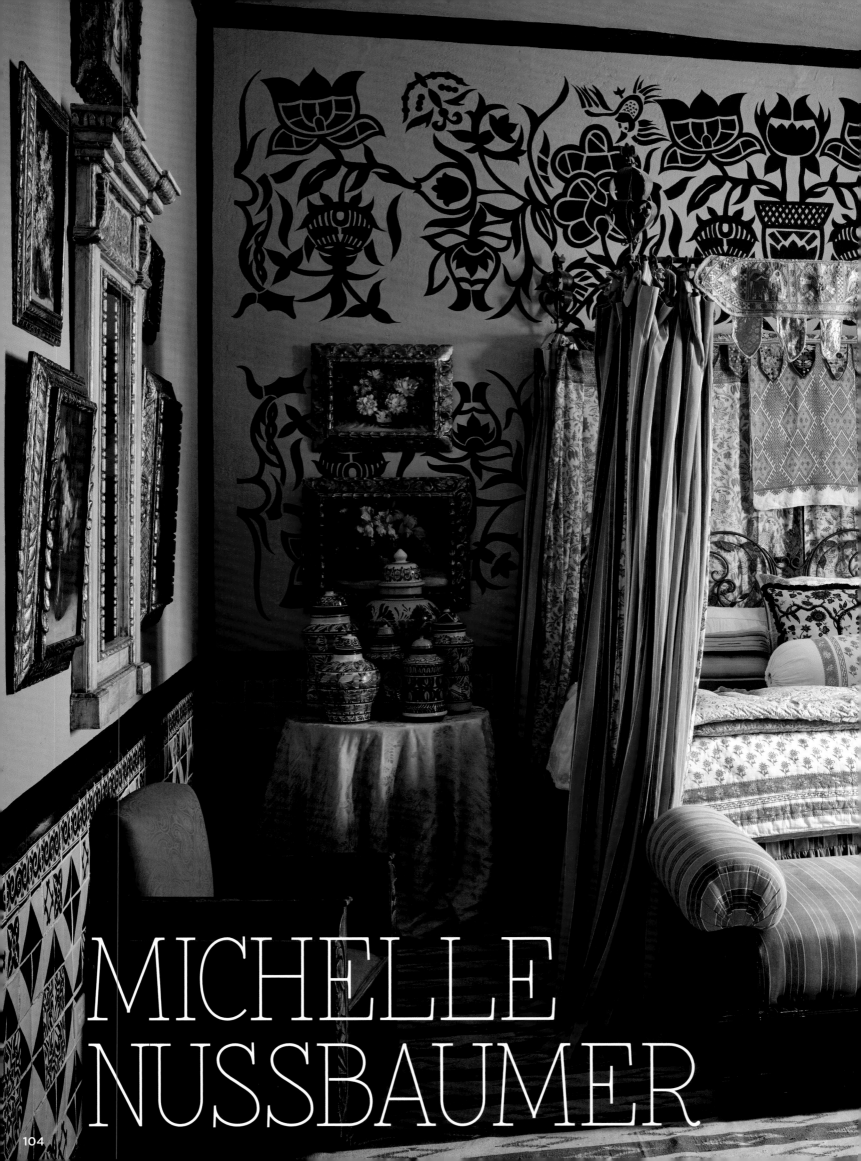

MICHELLE
NUSSBAUMER

Designer: Michelle Nussbaumer.
Company: Ceylon et Cie, Dallas, USA. Turning Old World inspiration into modern, soulful interiors, from private homes to boutique stores and luxury hotels. Current projects include a family compound in Laguna Beach, CA, a beach villa estate in Cabo, San Lucas, and a hacienda in West Texas. Recent work includes Slocum Warehouse in Dallas, San Miguel, Michelle's own home in Mexico, and the Dallas Goop pop-up for Gwyneth Paltrow.
Design philosophy: passionate about setting the stage for adventurous lives.

COLETTE VAN DEN THILLART

Designer: Colette van den Thillart. **Company:** Colette van den Thillart Interior Design, Toronto, Canada. Current projects include a residence in Rome, private residences in Toronto, an oceanfront condo in Miami and a Mid Century modern heritage refurbishment. Recent work includes a number of apartments, family homes and an executive office in Toronto, as well as residences in the UK, New York, and Los Angeles. **Design philosophy:** uplifting and experiential.

ARRCC

Designers: Mark Rielly, Jon Case, Michele Rhoda.
Company: ARRCC, Cape Town, South Africa. An acclaimed studio, specialising in residential, hospitality and leisure interiors worldwide. Current work includes a 14,000 sq. m. family home in Dubai, an exclusive line of floating villas in collaboration with SAOTA and Admares, and the refurbishment of an existing townhouse in Belgravia, London. Recent projects include an opulent penthouse in the newly developed Zaha Hadid building, One Thousand Museum, Miami, a contemporary home in the pine woods on an island in the Moskva River, Moscow, and a luxury safari lodge in the Sabi Sand Game Reserve, South Africa. **Design philosophy:** to create life enhancing interiors.

WU LICHENG

Designer: Wu Licheng.
Company: HYMC Architectural Engineering Design Co. Ltd. Guangzhou, China. Specialising in public space design, restaurants, hotels, clubs and crossover creative art works. Recent projects include Cai whisky bar, Four Seasons restaurant and Zhenxiang Chinese restaurant. Recent work includes Xiaoyu Hot pot, Régal Bistro French dessert bar, and a private house at Bailucang Hot springs. **Design philosophy:** insist on originality, break the constraints of our times, and express true emotion.

KATHARINE POOLEY

Designer: Katharine Pooley. **Company:** Katharine Pooley Ltd, London, UK. Encompassing a multitude of architectural genres and locations, her designs are renowned for their beauty, luxurious eclecticism and originality. Current projects include Chateau de la Croix des Gardes overlooking the bay of Cannes, a super yacht and a ground breaking residential development in Monaco. Recent work includes a palatial villa in Kuwait, a sleek and contemporary private residence overlooking Discovery Bay in Hong Kong and a chalet in Zermatt. **Design philosophy:** strive to be extraordinary.

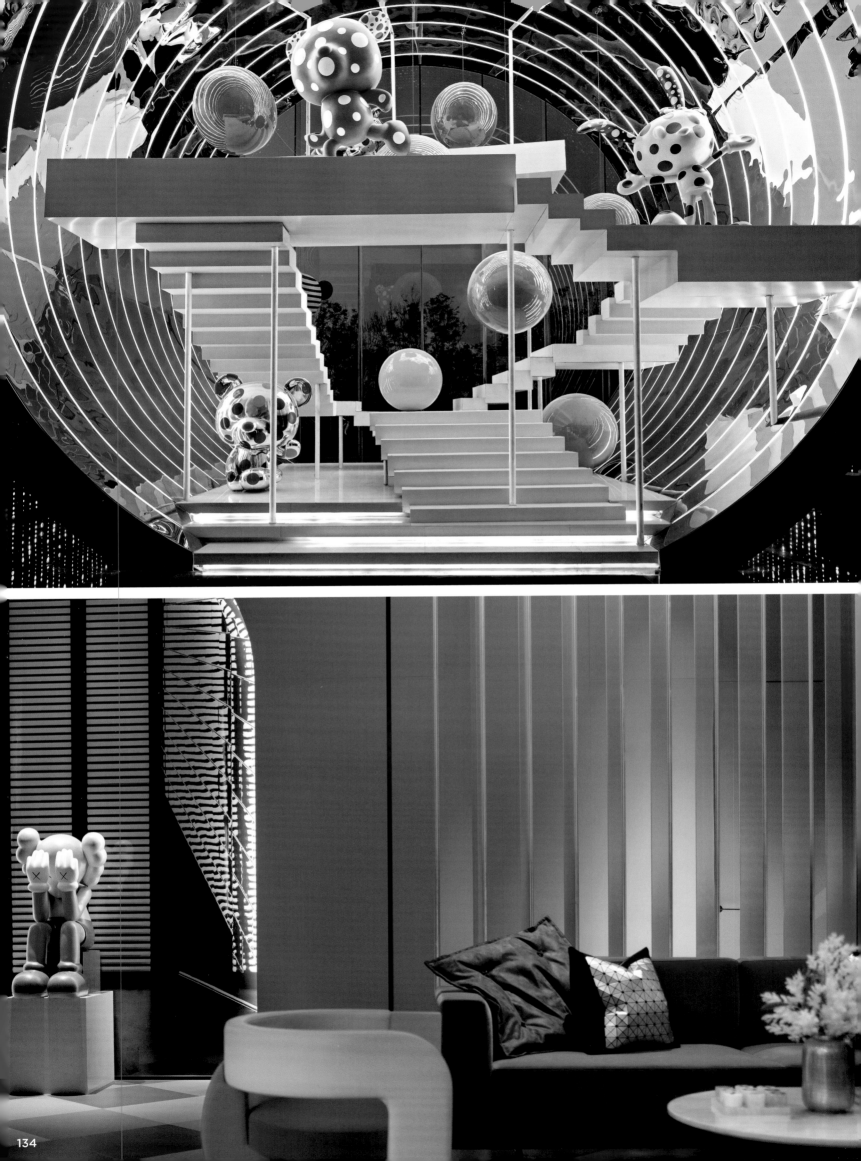

COO STAR
MANSION
COO
STAR
COMANSION

Life is
like a box of
chocolates.
you never
know what
you're going
to get.

MATRIXING

Designer: David Yu. **Company:** Matrixing, Shanghai, China. Founded in 2010, focused on the innovative design of real estate, turning traditional sales centres into a life experience to revitalise the community. Recent projects include multi functional sales centres in Guangzhou, City Exhibition Hall in Shenzhen, and the remodel of a sales centre in Shanghai. Current projects include a community library in Wuhan, CIFI brand showroom in Guangzhou and Glassy Box in Wuhan. **Design philosophy:** returning to the East.

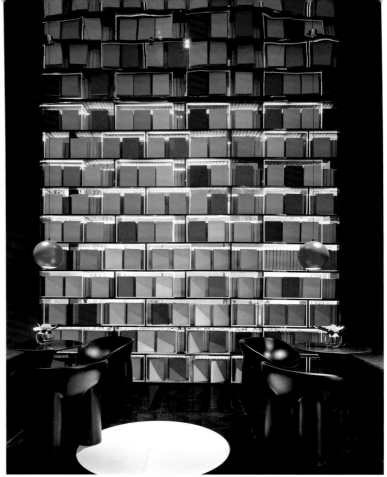

ATELIER
NINI
ANDRADE
SILVA

Designer: Nini Andrade Silva. **Company:** Atelier Nini Andrade Silva, Lisbon, Portugal. A luxury interior design studio covering residential, hospitality, offices, institutions, retail, food and beverage. Current projects include W São Paulo Hotel & Residences in Brazil, Hotel Hilton Porto Gaia in Portugal and a private residence in Chelsea Square, London. Recent work includes the VIP Lounge Lisbon Airport. the impressive Savoy Palace Hotel on Madeira Island and the magnificent Villa Foz Hotel & Spa in Porto. **Design philosophy:** 'I don't follow trends, I seek to create them.'

CHANG CHING-PING

Designer: Chang, Ching-Ping. **Company:** Tienfun Interior Planning, Taiwan, China. Luxury interior architecture in China and overseas, including private homes, luxury residential developments and boutique hotels. Current projects include a sales centre for Donde Tianyu in Wuhan, Queena Plaza Hotel in Tainan, Taiwan, and residential interior design at Treasure Garden in Taichung, Taiwan.
Design philosophy: extravagance in new Orientalism.

KELLY
HOPPEN

Designer: Kelly Hoppen CBE. **Company:** Kelly Hoppen Interiors, London, UK. Multi award winning interior designer with an extensive portfolio of multi faceted interiors, including luxury residential properties, private homes, yachts, private jets, 5 star resort & hotels and various commercial projects. Recent work includes a luxury penthouse in Australia, a 5 star hotel in Mauritius and several turnkey properties in Chengdu, China. Current projects include various private properties in the UK, a private residence in Monaco and a luxury cruise ship. **Design philosophy:** a fusion of clean lines, textures, layers and neutral tones, balanced with an opulent warmth.

NB STUDIO

Designer: Natalia Belonogova.
Company: NB-studio, Moscow, Russia. Specialising in the interior design for restaurants, boutique hotels and private homes since 2005. Recent projects include three restaurants and a private apartment in Moscow. Current work includes boutique hotels in the South of France and Moscow, five restaurants in Moscow, two in Kiev, and one in New York. **Design philosophy:** to create emotional and happy experiences.

Designer: Xie Peihe **Company:** AD Architecture, Shenzhen, China. Architectural and interior design from unique perspectives. Dedicated to creating distinctive visual art for each project. Current work includes WU Club, GENTLE L by Alan Yu, and the Novacolor paint showroom. Recent projects include Wu Club, Shenzhen and the Beijing and Shanghai, Xiao Da Dong, Roast Duck restaurants. **Design philosophy:** sensitivity and originality.

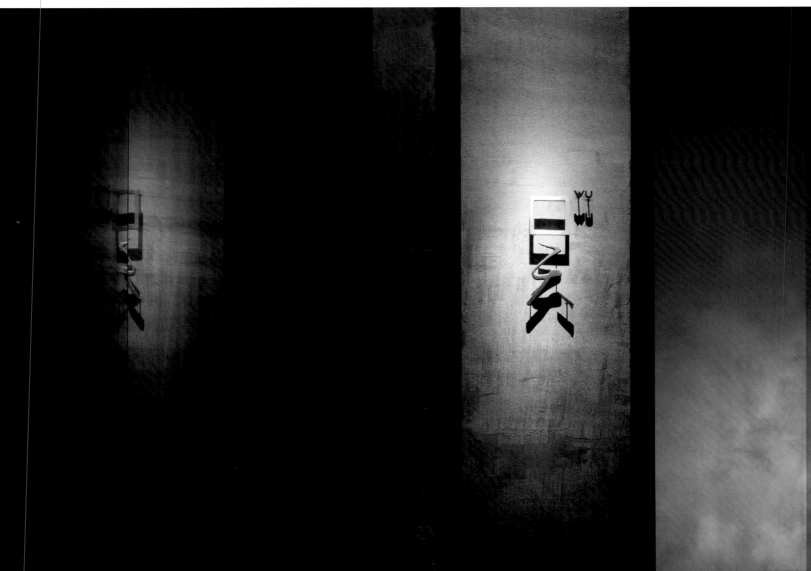

AD ARCHITECTURE

PATRICK SUTTON

Designer: Patrick Sutton. **Company:** Patrick Sutton, Baltimore, USA. A leader in the luxury interior design industry, Patrick opened the practice in 1994. His work has been widely published, his project Sagamore Pendry, was named the #1 Hotel in America by Conde Nast Traveler's 2018 Readers Choice Awards. Current work includes a new 15,000 sq. ft. ocean front shingle style home in Rehoboth, DE, a contemporary house renovation and addition for a design centric owner in Washington, DC, and an anchor restaurant interior for a new mixed use development project in Houston, TX. Recent projects include Maximon, Latin American restaurant in The Four Seasons Hotel in Baltimore, Choptank seafood restaurant in the historic Broadway Market in Fells Point Maryland, and a private 25,000 sq. ft. residence in Potomac, Maryland. **Design philosophy:** 'to tell the story of our clients' hopes, dreams and aspirations.'

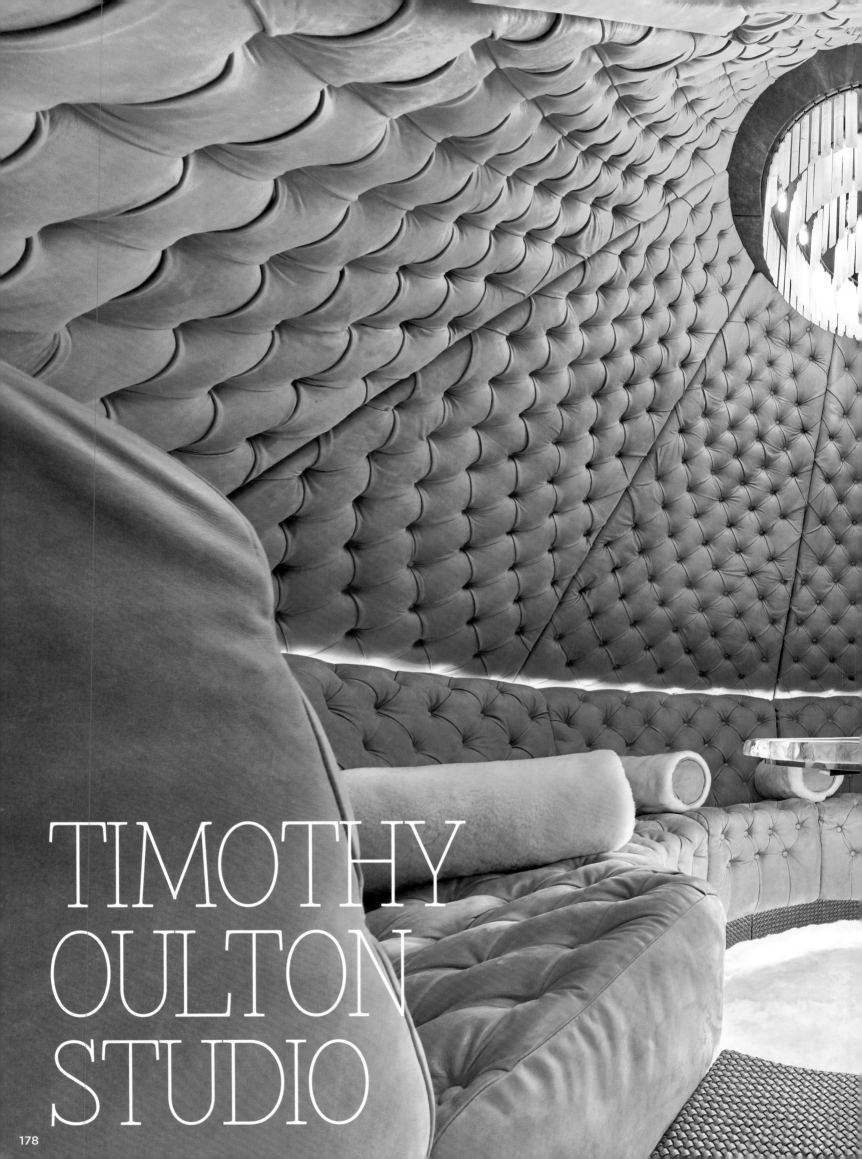

TIMOTHY
OULTON
STUDIO

Designers: Tim Oulton & Simon Laws. **Company:** Timothy Oulton Studio Ltd, London, UK. A multi disciplinary design practice, specialising in hospitality and retail to residential and workplaces, creating spaces with a unique point of view that centre around the art of hosting. Current projects include a London Pub, a café in the heart of the Grand Bazaar in Istanbul, and a private members club in Guangzhou. Recent work includes a wine club and restaurant in South East China, a private luxury residence in Alibag, and an Izakaya inspired Japanese restaurant opening in New Delhi. **Design philosophy:** visceral experiences with authentic materials.

PELIZZARI STUDIO

Designers: Claudia Pelizzari & David Morini. **Company:** Pelizzari Studio, Milan/Brescia, Italy. An architecture and interior design studio with projects including high end residences, the restoration of historic buildings, boutique hotels and restaurants in Italy and abroad. Current work includes villas on Lake Garda, a penthouse in the heart of Rome, the renovation of a building on the Grand Canal in Venice and a boutique hotel in a 17th century building in Northern Italy. Recent projects include two restaurants for a Milanese group active in hospitality, luxury apartments in Milan Citylife, in the building designed by Zaha Hadid, and the renovation of a farmhouse in the Padua countryside. **Design philosophy:** timeless elegance.

Designer: Angelos Angelopoulos. **Company:** Angelos Angelopoulos Associates Design+, Athens, Greece. Offering a bespoke concept to installation service for private clients, commercial projects, hotels, spas, gastronomy spaces, clubs and event venues. Recent work includes a sea resort hotel & spa set in 200 acres in Crete, with 300 bedrooms, 50 suites, gym, spa, restaurants and pool area, a business city hotel in Crete, a group of villas with a pool overlooking the Ionian Sea, and a boutique hotel in Rhodes Island. Current projects include a 9 bedroom private residence in Mykonos, with unique 180° sunset view, indoor breakfast bar, spa, hammam, pool, bar, outdoor cinema, spa, sauna and gym, all the suites of a Cycladic luxury boutique hotel, an eccentric, 1500 sq. m. Athens plateau residence hosting a huge gentlemen's only cigar room and collection of 50 Rolls & Bentley cars, a private residence with subterranean swimming pool and lounge area also in Athens, and a boutique hotel with luxury suites in Folegandros island. **Design philosophy:** holistic, integrated, life enhancing.

ANGELOS ANGELOPOULOS

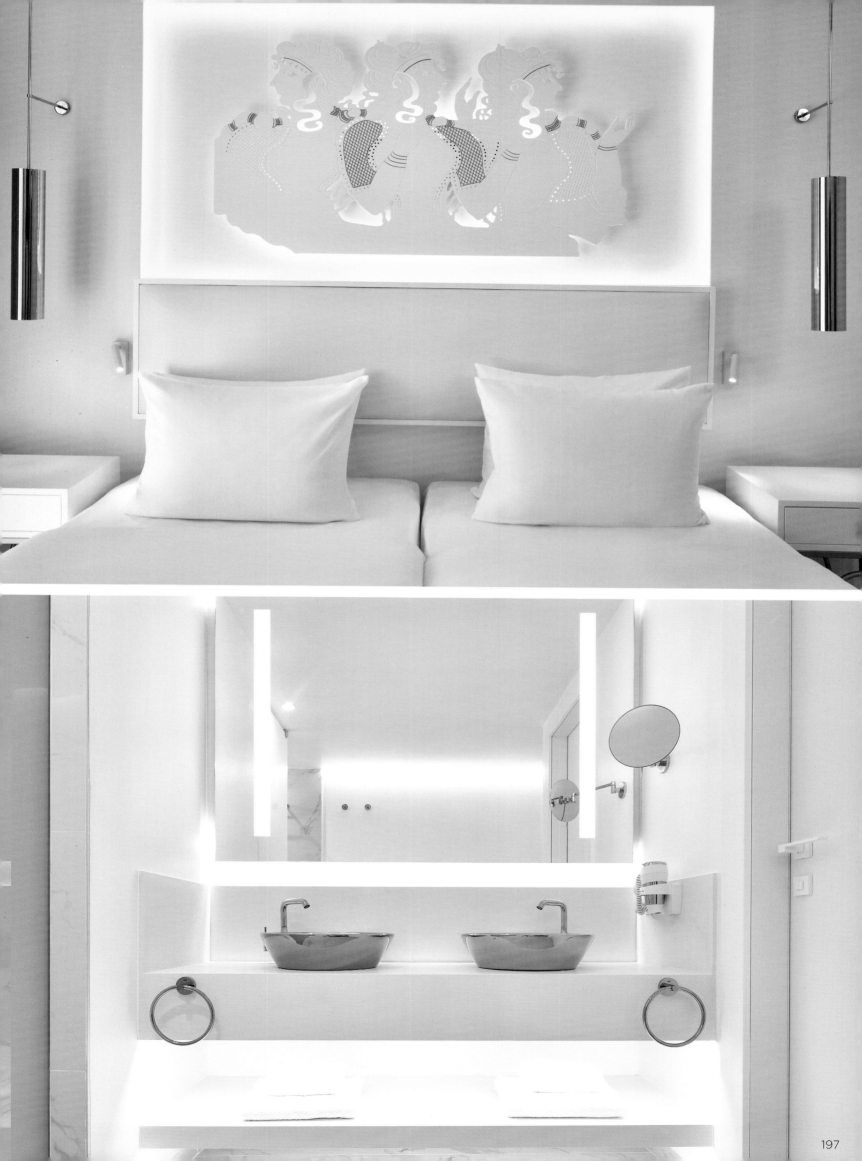

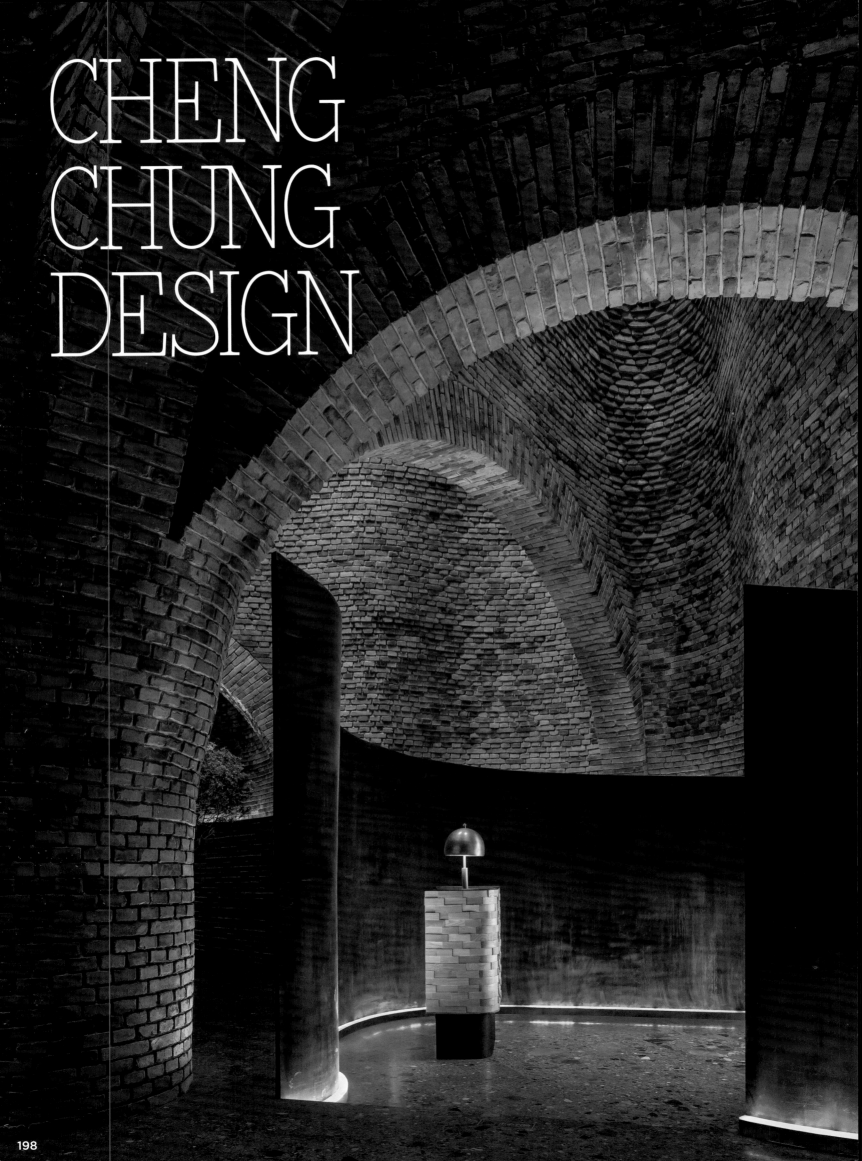

CHENG
CHUNG
DESIGN

Designers: Joe Cheng, Ken Hu, Aiden Du. **Company:** Cheng Chung Design (HK) Ltd, China. Experts in the hospitality design field; architectural & interior design, covering hotel, corporate, commercial complex, and residential. Current projects include a resort on the Shenzhen coastline, a golf resort in a historic Chinese city and a hotel conceived by several groups of distinctive red brick buildings in a folk town. Recent work includes a quadrangle courtyard house style hotel in Beijing, a hot spring resort and a resort surrounded by magnificent lake scenery in Suzhou. **Design philosophy:** Eastern artistic conception in Western form.

Designer: Ekaterina Iakovenko. **Company:** JP Interior Design, Moscow, Russia. Providing bespoke solutions. Current projects include a luxury apartment in Malaga, Spain, a private 1300 sq. m. family residence with contemporary Art Deco interiors, terrace and pool, on the prestigious 300 hectare Agalarov estate outside Moscow, and a classically designed, 600 sq. m. private family house. **Design philosophy:** light, decorative, individual.

JP INTERIORS

GREG NATALE

GREG NATALE

Designer: Greg Natale. **Company:** Greg Natale Design, Sydney, Australia. Specialising in architecture and interior design for luxury residential and commercial spaces in Australia as well as internationally. Current projects include a harbourside Mosman house inspired by Milan's Villa Necchi Campiglio, a historic homestead in country Victoria, and the new Greg Natale Design headquarters and residence in inner city Darlinghurst, located in a former stable. Recent work includes a sprawling staff headquarters for a major retail brand in regional Victoria, a modern palazzo style house on the Brisbane River, and a penthouse apartment beside the Sydney Harbour Bridge. **Design philosophy:** tailored, sophisticated, layered, embracing bold colour and pattern.

JENNIFER GARRIGUES

Designer: Jennifer Garrigues. **Company:** Jennifer Garrigues Interior Design, Palm Beach, USA. Specialising in residential projects. Recent work includes a new build with beautiful views, a garden with outdoor loggia for entertaining in North Palm Beach, a complete renovation on Jupiter Island, Florida, and a large renovation in North Palm Beach. Current work includes a magnificent duplex in the West Village, New York City, with a terrace looking over the Hudson River and Statue of Liberty, a new build with beautiful landscaping in North Palm Beach, and a complete rebuild with golf course views, also in North Palm Beach. **Design philosophy:** elegant, exotic global chic.

FRANKIE FAN

Designer: Frankie Fan. **Company:** D+Design Office, Beijing, Shanghai, Shenzhen, Wuhan & Chengdu, China. High end commercial and private residential. Current projects include a Great Ice and Snow World Snowy Kingdom for Blue Town in Hangzhou, an exhibition centre for Corporate Avenue 1 in Wuhan and Beijing Li Palace villa. Recent work includes a children's museum at China Children's Centre, Suzhou Vanke Sky park sales centre and a River View penthouse in Wuhan. **Design philosophy:** symbiosis in space, city, ecology, community.

I LOVE THIS GAME.

STEFANO DORATA

Designer: Stefano Dorata. **Company:** Studio Dorata, Rome, Italy. An architectural practice for apartments, hotels, villas and yachts in Europe, North and South America, Middle & Far East. Current projects include a building in Coppedè, Rome, a house in Rimini, and a hotel in Ostuni, Southern Italy. Recent work includes a house in Jaffa, Tel Aviv, an apartment in Lungotevere, Rome, and a family house on Ponza island. **Design philosophy:** to seek the 'excitement' element in each project.

CHRIS GODDARD

Designers: Chris Goddard. **Company:** Goddard Design Group, Springdale, AR, USA. Internationally awarded, luxury residential and commercial practice that specialise in creating timeless interiors steeped in storytelling. Current projects include a luxury penthouse on Seven Mile Beach, Grand Cayman, a monumental stone and glass residence at Little Rock, Arkansas and a lakeside compound with grounds and boathouse in Texas. Recent work includes a residence in Palm Beach, a mountain chalet in Aspen, and a historic riverside retreat in Fayetteville, Arkansas. **Design philosophy:** timeless elegance.

LI XIANG

Designer: Li Xiang. **Company:** X+Living Architectural Design, Shanghai, China. Specialising in interior architecture mostly in China including retail stores, entertainment venues, offices, boutique hotels, restaurants. Current projects include a kindergarten in Zhejiang, a flagship store for a major food company in Shanghai and a shopping mall in Guangxi. Recent work includes Dujiangyan Zhongshuge bookstore in Sichuan, a playground in Guangdong, and a cinema in Shanxi. **Design philosophy:** embracing a worldview to seek a new paradigm to amaze.

ELICYON

Designer: Charu Gandhi. **Company:** Elicyon, London, UK. Founded in 2014 and based in their studio in Kensington. In 2020 Elicyon completed a number of landmark projects across London in both private homes and leading developments including Chelsea Barracks, Lancaster Gate, Mayfair Park Residences and a new boutique development in Beaufort Gardens, Knightsbridge, as well as international projects in Dubai and Kuwait. Current projects include a 5 bedroom apartment in One Hyde Park, Salt, a penthouse apartment in Marylebone and a palatial home in Saudi Arabia. Recent work includes a penthouse apartment in One Palm, Dubai, two apartment units in a Beaufort Street townhouse and a three bedroom apartment in Mayfair. **Design philosophy:** storytelling lies at the heart of Elicyon' s company ethos.

LUCAS/EILERS DESIGN

Designers: Sandra Lucas & Sarah Eilers. **Company:** Lucas/Eilers Design Associates, Houston, USA. Creating timeless, thoughtful interiors relevant to their clients' diverse tastes and personalities. Current projects include a substantial vacation home in Bristol, Rhode Island, a 1940's ranch compound in West Texas, and a multi level fishing cabin in Crested Butte. Recent work includes an estate in Virginia, a vacation home on Kiawah Island, an art collector's home in Houston, and homes around Houston, set amid rolling hills and endless sky. **Design philosophy:** tailor made designs from inception to installation.

GANG CAO

Designers: Gang Cao. **Company:** Henan Erheyong Architectural Decoration Design, Zhengzhou, China. Specialising in small buildings, high end private residential, hotel and commercial design. Current projects include Chang'an ancient village in Zhengzhou, including its hotels and restaurants, major hotels in the mountains of Yichuan and Guanjing and high end residential in Zhengzhou. Recent work includes architecture, landscape and the interior design of Zhengzhou real estate sales centre, the renovation of old houses in Dongpo Village and the interior design of courtyard houses in high rise buildings in Zhengzhou. **Design philosophy:** space design following nature and the heart.

JEFFREYS
INTERIORS

Designers: Georgina Fraser, Jo Aynsley.
Company: Jeffreys Interiors, Edinburgh, Scotland. Reflecting the tastes, lifestyle and character of their clients, this versatile team specialise in unique, stylish residential and commercial projects across Scotland and the UK. Current projects include a newly built boutique hotel in Northumberland, a modern new build in the Scottish Highlands & commercial office premises for a start up drinks distribution company. Recent work includes a 17th century mansion in East Lothian, two distinct townhouses on Edinburgh's Ann Street, and a unique wedding venue near Alnwick.
Design philosophy: your taste, our talent.

Designer: Allison Paladino. **Company:** Allison Paladino Interior Design & Collections, Florida, USA. A boutique practice specialising in custom interior architecture and furnishings, down to the last accessory. Allison is also a product designer with Perennials, Visual Comfort, Century Furniture, Fine Art Handcrafted Lighting, EJ Victor, as well as a Ghost designer for McGuire. Current projects include an ocean front estate and various homes in Palm Beach, a Jupiter residence in Palm Beach Gardens and an apartment in New York. **Design philosophy:** unique, understated, serene.

ALLISON PALADINO

Designer: Nicky Dobree. **Company:** Nicky Dobree Interior Design, London, UK. Specialising in luxury ski chalets and private residential interiors internationally. Current projects include a pair of iconic chalets in Val d'Isere, a New England style house by the sea, the renovation of a London Mews and a chalet in Switzerland. Recent work includes a barn conversion in Buckinghamshire, a large family house in London and several chalets across the French Alps. **Design philosophy:** timeless elegance.

NICKY DOBREE

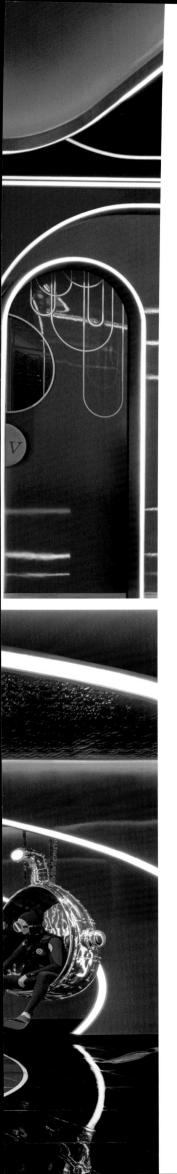

LIN XU

Designer: Xu Lin. **Company:** SPACE^3 INTERIOR DESIGN, ShenYang, China. Specialising in high end entertainment design. Current work includes a restaurant bar & KTV complex in Los Angeles, Stage KTV in Boston and Gramy KTV in Shenzhen. Recent projects include Guiyang Anna KTV, Foshan MIX KTV, and Guangzhou MIX KTV. **Design philosophy:** art and entertainment.

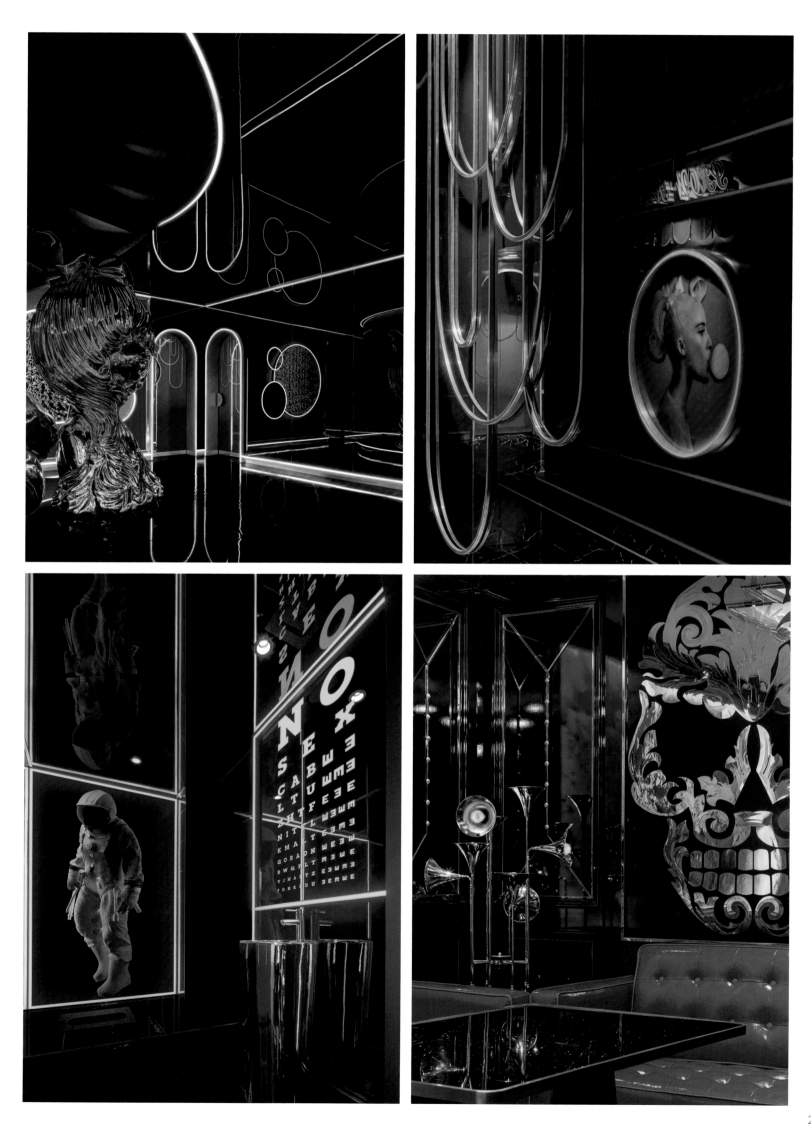

JOANA ARANHA STUDIO

Designer: Joana Aranha, architect Marta Aranha.
Company: Joana Aranha Studio, Lisbon, Portugal. Specialising in luxury interior design and architecture with a creative vocation and multidisciplinary approach, for residential, corporate, commercial, hospitality, yachts and private jets. Current projects include a villa in Quinta do Lago, Algarve, several private houses in Comporta, and a family residence in Galway, Ireland. Recent work includes a manor house in Lumiar, Lisbon, a country house in Évora, Alentejo, and a private house in New Delhi, India. **Design philosophy:** extraordinary living for extraordinary people.

JANIE MOLSTER DESIGNS

Designer: Janie Molster. **Company:** Janie Molster Designs, Richmond, VA, USA. A full service interior design firm working across the U.S. and specialising in contemporary residential design as well as historic renovations. Current projects include an expansive oceanfront family compound on the West coast of Florida, a historic renovation of a mid 1700's plantation home in the Virginia countryside, and a Palm Beach oceanfront pied-à-terre. Recent work includes a renovation and redesign of the Sayre House at the Washington National Cathedral, Wasington, DC, the Early Mountain Winery event spaces, dining, and tasting room, Madison, Virginia, the renovation of a 1920's riverfront Georgian manse in Richmond, Virginia. **Design philosophy:** with a respect for the past and traditional architecture, we like to straddle the boundaries of many contemporary design genres; 'I'm not guided by genre, period, or pedigree. I am guided by good.'

281

WU WENLI

Designer: Wu WenLi. **Company:** Huge Rock Design, Shenzhen, China. Providing a professional interior design service for sales centres, show homes, villas, clubhouses, commercial and public spaces, for real estate developers and commercial investors. Current projects include a villa in Fuzhou, a hotel in Guizhou, and a sales centre in Nanning. Recent work includes sales centres in Yiyang and Wenling, as well as a clubhouse in Fuzhou. **Design philosophy:** contextualism: omni-directional space experience.

ROSA MAY SAMPAIO

Designer: Rosa May Sampaio. **Company:** Rosa May Arquitetura de Interiores, São Paulo, Brazil. Predominantly classic, yet contemporary statement interiors. Current projects include a house in São Paulo, a pavilion in a country house in São Paulo, a penthouse in Rio de Janeiro, a new build cottage and a swimming pool on a farm in the South of Brazil. Recent work includes a village house. **Design philosophy:** scale, proportion, geometry, elegance, harmony.

COISA, COUSA s.f. 'AQUILO QUE
EXISTE OU PODE EXISTIR' 'OBJE
TO INANIMADO' COUSSA XVIII,
XIII, coysa XVI IDO lat. causa

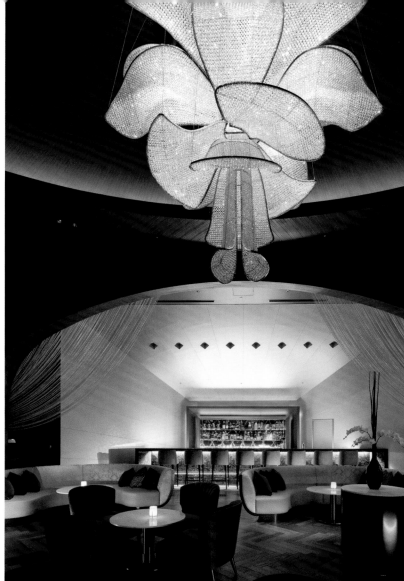

KKS GROUP

Designers: Ryo Aoyagi, Makiko Goto, Naohiro Yoshida, Masahiro Kaihoko, Akemi Kato, Satsuki Nagashima. **Company:** KKS GROUP (Kanko Kikaku Sekkeisha), Tokyo, Japan. An architecture and interior design practice specialising in hospitality design since 1962. Current projects include Hyatt Place Kyoto, Hotel Indigo Inuyama, and Hotel Okura Vladivostok, Russia. Recent work includes The Okura Hotel, Japan, the banquet area of Teppanyaki restaurant, a Chinese restaurant, Westin Miyako Hotel Kyoto, and The Barracks Hotel Sentosa, Singapore.
Design philosophy: "不易流行" (Hueki-Ryuko) (a word based in Haiku) meaning 'there are things which don't change or shouldn't change, but we should still keep adopting new air and updating ourselves.

STUDIO MHNA

Designers: Marc Hertrich & Nicolas Adnet. **Company:** Studio MHNA, Paris, France. For 30 years the studio has designed projects mixing functionality and aesthetics, fantasy, luxury and poetry. Current work includes the complete refurbishment of the Constance Halaveli resort & spa in the Maldives, a luxury residential project in Geneva, and the entire renovation of Château de Frefossé in Etretat, France. Recent projects includes the creation of a Mövenpick Hotel and art gallery in Abidjan, Ivory Coast, a new concept store for Caviar Petrossian in Paris, and a rooftop restaurant at the White Palm Hotel in Cannes. **Design philosophy:** listen carefully, be creative.

BENJAMIN JOHNSTON DESIGN

Designer: Benjamin Johnston. **Company:** Benjamin Johnston Design, Houston, USA. Award winning, internationally published architecture and design firm specialising in luxury residential, commercial and hospitality. Current projects include a cliffside coastal home in California, a penthouse and multiple lake homes in Austin, and a 25,000 sq.ft. chateau in Houston. Recent work includes the renovation of a historic townhouse in Georgetown, Washington D.C, an apartment overlooking NYC's Central Park, a luxury skincare salon in Beverly Hills, and the complete reimagination of common spaces within the 50 story Warwick Tower high rise in Houston. **Design philosophy:** Classic. Curated. Cool. ™

Designers: Chen Yi, XiaoFeng, Chen Ming, Lu Kunquan **Company:** Nanjing Matilian Space Design, China. A diverse creative service agency integrating high end private house design and renovation, commercial spaces and real estate projects. Current work includes villas in Nanjing, including Poly 24, Masland, and Yiyun Valley. Recent work includes Nanjing Taiheyuanzi villa, Nanjing Zhengdajiujiantang villa, and Nanjing vanke anpin garden villa. **Design philosophy:** design promotes residential happiness.

NANJING MATILIAN SPACE DESIGN

DONALD NXUMALO

Designer: Donald Nxumalo. **Company:** Donald Nxumalo Interior Design, Sandton, South Africa. Luxury interior design with a contemporary African aesthetic, delivered through collaborations, curated, branded and bespoke for the home, hotel and executive offices. Current projects include an impressive multi level home on the Atlantic seaboard, Cape Town, a five star boutique hotel, and a list of exclusive homes in Johannesburg, Cape Town and Zambia. Recent work includes a sea side villa in Durban, an impressive manor house in Sandhurst, Johannesburg and high end showhouses. **Design philosophy:** to create spaces where clients can truly be themselves.

COPPER & TIN

Designer: Elena Spiridonova & architect Roman Andrusenko.
Company: Copper & Tin, Moscow, Russia. With almost a decade in design, the studio has completed numerous projects overseas, including private apartments in Moscow and St Petersburg, a villa in Antibes, a chalet in Courchevel, a private residence in London and an apartment in Monaco. Current work includes several apartments in Moscow, a villa in St. Barts, a country house outside London and an office in Monaco. **Design philosophy:** 'much like a dance: we lead, require space'.

DENTON HOUSE
DESIGN STUDIO

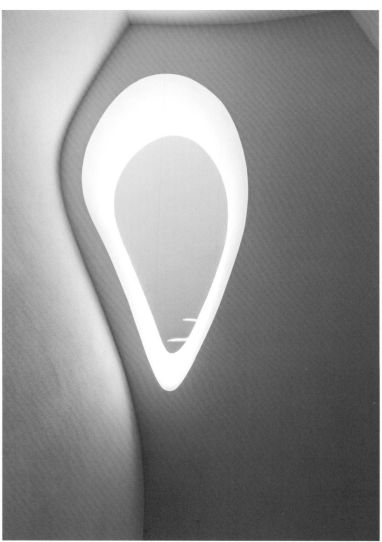

Designer: Rebecca Buchan. **Company:** Denton House, Salt Lake City, USA. An award winning interdisciplinary global design firm, with a team of over 100 employees and additional offices in New York, Las Vegas, Hawaii, and Cabo San Lucas. For more than 25 years, Denton House has created luxury designs and signature looks for clients worldwide. Current projects include the planning and development of a new luxurious community in the Wasatch Mountains, interiors for several custom homes in Cabo San Lucas, Hawaii, Deer Valley and Kentucky. Recent work includes several private residences in Mexico, a large estate in Montana and residences in Hawaii. **Design philosophy:** luxury designed for living.

SODA

evo

vivinevo PERFUMERY

Designers: Yuan Jiang & Chen Song. **Company:** SODA Architects, Beijing, China. Founded in 2016, providing intelligent solutions for urban spaces, commercial, residential and art installations, creating multisensory experiences. Current projects include a shopping area in the National Museum of China cultural products exhibition hall, the exhibition of POLY Auction, Design Spring, contemporary Chinese furniture design fair. Recent work includes commercial space in Beijing, an exhibition hall in China International Import Expo in Shanghai and a restaurant bar in Beijing. **Design philosophy:** connect the virtual world and the real world by design.

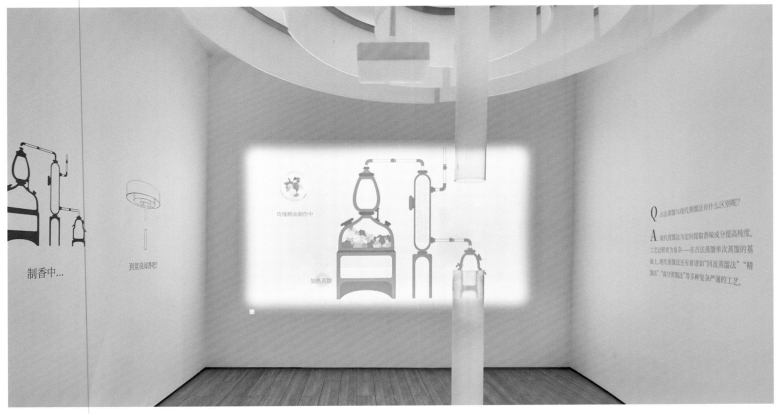

香感觉醒·可以互动的香容器
让空间装地香水的流动，让鼻子带口探索，寻访古香史的根脉追思。
参与触摸明的感官互动，与大师的调香艺术面对面，用汉译式的体验
致敬香氛艺术，唤醒每个人的香感。

vivinevo PERFUMERY
维维尼奥香氛艺术馆

MARI VATTEKAR MARKMAN

Designer: Mari Vattekar Markman. **Company:** Vattekar Markman Interiørarkitektur, Norway & Sweden. Full scale residential and secondary home projects, especially period homes in Scandinavia. Current projects include an apartment in central Stockholm, a summer house in the Oslofjord and a Swedish Grace villa in Stockholm. Recent work includes a large family residence in Oslo, a chic pied-à-terre in central Stockholm and a farmhouse in Southern Norway. **Design philosophy:** sophisticated, comfortable, life enhancing.

JORGE CAÑETE

Designer: Jorge Cañete. **Company:** Interior Design Philosophy, Vaud, Switzerland. A personal approach to design, taking inspiration from the environment, the location and the client. Recent work includes a gourmet boutique, a restaurant in a monastery, the creation of a lamp collection and the curating of several solo shows. Current projects include various residential projects, including the renovation of a medieval house in Switzerland, a private apartment overlooking Lake Luzern and the creation of a contemporary art gallery. **Design philosophy:** enchanting interiors with a narrative and poetic philosophy.

TOMOKO IKEGAI

Designer: Tomoko Ikegai. **Company:** ikg inc. Tokyo, Japan. Established in 2006, ikg is known for its comprehensive design services and highly tailored spaces. Tomoko is not only a designer, but an acclaimed creative director working on large developments based on a solid branding concept. Current projects include a members' club and restaurants in Ginza, Tokyo, a commercial complex in Beijing, and a large scale renovation for a condominium in Hiroo, Tokyo. Recent work includes the lobby of a new headquarters for a trading company, the showrooms, common area entrance lobby and lounge of a condominium in Nishiazabu, and two luxurious condominium renovations in Tokyo. **Design philosophy:** value which lasts.

SUZANNE LOVELL

Designer: Suzanne Lovell. **Company:** Suzanne Lovell Inc, Chicago, USA. Licensed architects, interior designers, art advisors and business professionals who deliver a fully integrated design experience. Current projects include a 15,000 sq. ft. penthouse with sweeping panoramic views of the Gulf Coast in Naples, FL, a multi generational compound spanning three lots in Highland Park, IL, and a Balinese inspired new build right on the water on Captiva Island, FL. Recent work includes a low country family residence on the ocean on Hilton Head Island, SC, a landmarked Howard Van Doren Shaw residence in Oak Park, IL, and a sprawling vacation residence atop the cliffs overlooking Lake Michigan in Lakeside, MI. **Design philosophy:** couture residential environments for extraordinary living.

HARE + KLEIN

Designer: Meryl Hare. **Company:** Hare + Klein, Sydney, Australia. Specialising in bespoke residential interior design in Australia and overseas. Current projects include luxurious apartments in the Eastern Suburbs of Sydney, several large residential projects in Sydney, a beach house in South Australia, a penthouse in China, and a rural property in NSW. Recent work includes a major redesign of a cliff top home overlooking the Pacific Ocean in Sydney, a beach house in Pearl Beach NSW, a historic, harbourside home in Sydney's Northshore, a major renovation of an Eastern Suburbs home, as well as several penthouses and apartments. **Design philosophy:** to enrich lives through design.

STEVE LEUNG

Designer: Steve Leung. **Company:** Steve Leung Design Group, Hong Kong, China. One of the largest interior design practices in Asia, and the first ever to be listed on the Hong Kong Stock Exchange (SEHK: 2262). Providing high end architectural, interior and product design in over 100 cities worldwide. Current projects include luxury serviced apartments and hotel rooms for Address Harbour Point in Dubai Creek, an upscale Chinese restaurant for the Mandarin Oriental in Ho Chi Minh, Vietnam and eco-friendly residences for a Smart and Sustainable Eco-city in Phnom Penh, Cambodia. Recent works include McDonald's CUBE flagship restaurants in Chengdu and Shenzhen, SLD+, SLD's Corporate Culture Centre in Shanghai, and The Londoner Hotel & The St. Regis Bar in Macao SAR, China. **Design philosophy:** Design Without Limits.

NEHA & SACHIN GUPTA

Designers: Neha Gupta & Sachin Gupta. **Company:** Beyond Designs, New Delhi, India. Specialising in luxury, residential interior design in India, as well as retailing bespoke furniture, lighting, lifestyle accessories and bespoke artwork. Current projects include a beach villa in Chennai, a farmhouse in Jaipur, and a farmhouse in New Delhi. Recent work includes a city residence in Udaipur, a Pan Asian restaurant in New Delhi and a city house in Friends Colony, South Delhi. **Design philosophy:** Neoclassical fusion.

YOUNG HUH
INTERIOR DESIGN

Designer: Young Huh. **Company:** Young Huh Interior Design, New York City, USA. A full service design practice, specialising in high end residential and commercial projects across the globe, including private homes, boutique hotels, restaurants, corporate offices and aviation. Current projects include a large historic Tudor in Chicago, townhouse gut renovations both in Brooklyn Heights and the Upper West Side, a mountain home in Jackson Hole, a modern high rise apartment near Lincoln Centre, and an art studio and offices on the Upper West Side. Recent work includes a floor through apartment at 520 Park Avenue, an Easthampton home backing onto a nature reserve, and a gentleman's apartment off 5th Avenue on the Upper East Side. **Design philosophy:** resetting the design narrative for each project, with a touch of wanderlust.

100 INTERIORS
ROUND THE WORLD

ESCAPE

HOLIDAY

PATSY BLUNT INTERIORS

Designer: Patsy Blunt. **Company:** Patsy Blunt Interiors, Surrey, UK. An independent practice specialising in small, luxury developments, residential and commercial work, throughout the UK and abroad. Current projects include a villa in the Algarve, a ten bedroom 16th century property in Bedfordshire and a luxury apartment in Chelsea. Recent work includes a three bedroom apartment in Surrey, a family home on the Wentworth Estate and a holiday home in Palm Beach, Florida. **Design philosophy:** classic with a contemporary twist.

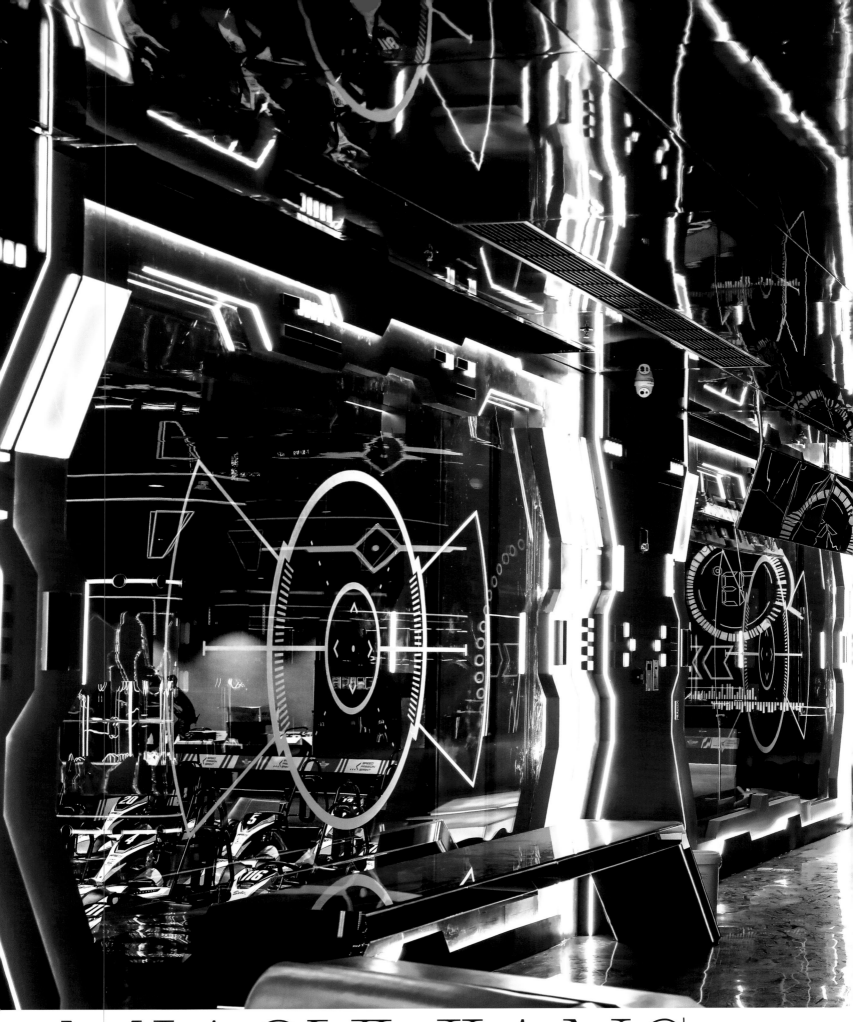

MIAOYI JIANG &

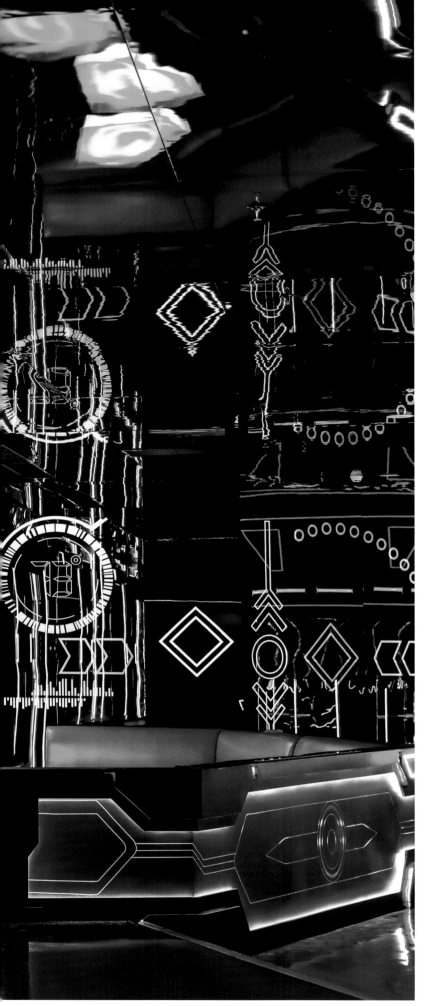

Designers: Miaoyi Jiang, Jianhong Pan.
Company: Gold Mantis Design, Shanghai, China. A comprehensive design company with a full industry design and construction services for hotels, offices, hospitality, medical, education and religion, all over the country. The company has been ranked among the Top 100 Decoration Companies in China. Current projects include boutique homestays in Xiangtan; Ningbo Zhiye Technology office building; Narada Hot Springs resort Luozhou; Beijing CITIC Tower; Kew Green Hotel Hongqiao Shanghai and Shanghai Lingang International Conference Centre. **Design philosophy:** inspiration comes from life.

JIANHONG PAN

PIPPA PATON

Designer: Pippa Paton. **Company:** Pippa Paton Design, Oxfordshire, UK. A boutique interior design and architecture studio specialising in the sympathetic transformation of period Cotswold homes for contemporary living. Current projects include a Grade II listed country house, a Grade II listed Edwardian farmhouse and a Grade II listed manor. Recent work includes a Grade II listed Palladian villa, a Grade II listed village house and a contemporary Oxfordshire house. **Design philosophy:** respect the past to create the future.

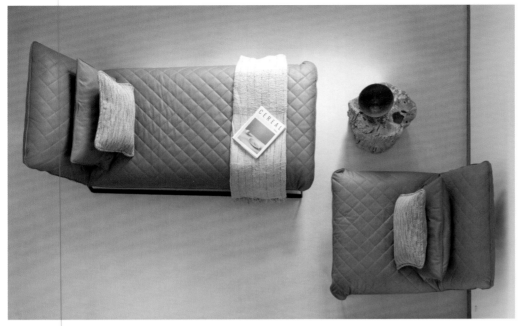

OLGA HANONO

Designer: Olga Hanono. **Company:** Olga Hoanono, Mexico City. Projects are international and iconic, including a curated Art House, a family villa on a vineyard in San Miguel de Allende, and a simple yet luxurious apartment project on Miami Beach. Recent work includes the creation of OH's own flooring collection, a collaboration on a lighting collection with a major European porcelain manufacturer, as well as the design of an Art Deco inspired private club in Rio. **Design philosophy:** to create a unique masterpiece in every project.

ROBERT KANER
INTERIOR DESIGN

Designer: Robert Kaner. **Company:** Robert Kaner Interior Design, New York, USA. Combining a modernist design approach with respect for history and an appreciation of gracious living. Specializing in residences in the New York region and around the United States. Current projects include a new build three story penthouse apartment with a contemporary interior, the renovation of a 1920's apartment with historic furnishings, and the redesign of a two story penthouse with contemporary, Mid Century and classic Italian design. Recent work includes the complete refurbishment of a home in The Hamptons, a coastal residence in Longboat Key, Florida, and the redesign of major rooms in an early 20th century coastal home in New Jersey. **Design philosophy:** a unique design language for each project, informed by the client and the surrounding architecture.

C&C DESIGN

Designer: Peng Zheng. **Company:** C&C Design Co. Ltd. Guangzhou, China. Founded in 2005, work includes hotels and offices, providing customers with a one stop service from architecture, design, interior design and display. Current projects include a marine themed marketing centre in Zhuhai, a large indoor integrated marketing centre in Guangzhou, and the renovation of an old building. **Design philosophy:** focus on the construction of space to make the design more inclusive.

星空之心·树立小镇精神标识
The heart of the starry sky and the spirit of the town

TAYLOR HOWES

Designer: Karen Howes. **Company:** Taylor Howes Designs, London, UK. Founded by Karen in 1993, Taylor Howes is a multi award winning, luxury interior design studio with a reputation for creating interiors of distinction. Providing turnkey residential interior design, interior architecture, project management and furniture design services for private individuals and property developers. Recent work includes an 18,000 sq. ft. new build country house in the Cotswolds, a 7 bedroom house in Knightsbridge, and a palace in Kuwait. Current projects include a 47 apartment super prime development in Knightsbridge, a boutique hotel in Soho and a 32,000 sq. ft. villa in Dubai. **Design philosophy:** as personalised as a work of art.

MEG LONERGAN INTERIORS

Designer: Meg Lonergan. **Company:** Meg Lonergan Interiors, Houston, USA. An award winning studio that embodies quintessential Southern style balanced by a vibrant international influence. Offering full service residential interior design services to clientele nationwide. Current projects include a mid century historic riverfront estate in Austin, Texas, a newly constructed contemporary ocean view residence in Pacific Palisades, California and a New Orleans inspired oyster/cocktail bar concept in Houston. Recent work includes a modern revamp of a historic residential estate in Houston, a substantial European modern country club home in Houston, and an art and antique driven second home on a Texas ranch. **Design philosophy:** a playful yet timeless approach, rooted in antiques and fine art.

PHILIP TANG
& BRIAN IP

THE
CAMPTON

Designers: Philip Tang & Brian Ip. **Company:** PTang Studio Ltd, Hong Kong, China. Specialising in luxury interior design in Hong Kong and the Asia Pacific region including residential developments and commercial projects. Current work includes a show house in Hong Kong, a residential development in Singapore and co-working office in Hong Kong. Recent projects include a sales office in Hong Kong, a residential development in the Philippines and show villas in Thailand. **Design philosophy:** modest, back to basics.

DÔME
INTERIORS

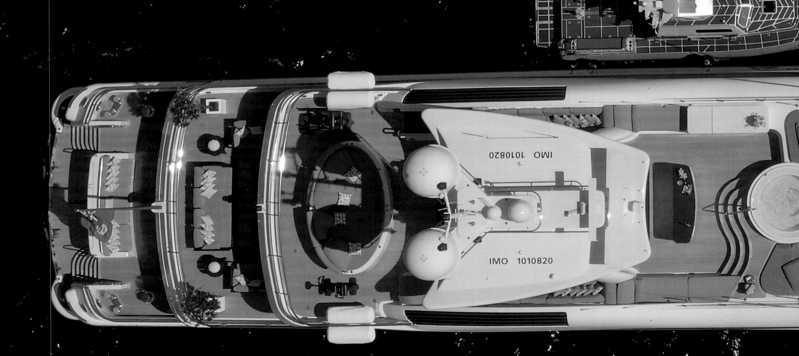

Designer: Cécile Demole. **Company:** Dôme Project Interiors, Geneva, Switzerland. A luxury interior architecture and design studio, specialising in the interiors of private residences, chalets and business premises. Current work includes the full renovation of a summer house in St. Tropez, a family house in Nassau, Bahamas, and an apartment in Geneva. Recent projects include the refit of an Amels yacht, a penthouse in Miami, and two apartments in Madrid. **Design philosophy:** passion, drive, detail.

YONG WANG

Designer: Yong Wang. **Company:** Beijing Wuxiang Space Architecture Design Studio, China. Covering brand consultancy, planning, architecture, interior design, environmental art design and decorative art consultancy for commercial real estate, hotels, resorts and custom corporate space. Current projects include TRT Zhima health store, FANUC office design and Qingniaoyunju B & B hotel. Recent work includes Beijing Xiaosong library, TRT Zhima leading health store, and Vanke commercial space renovation project. **Design philosophy:** dig the value behind the project.

JIMMIE MARTIN

Designers: Jimmie Karlsson & Martin Nihlmar. **Company:** Jimmie Martin, London, UK. Specialising in residential and commercial projects in the UK and overseas, as well as their own line of custom furniture and art. Current projects include a 6,500 sq. ft. country cottage conversion in Leicestershire, a high end tattoo studio in the West End, and a warehouse loft apartment in West London. Recent work includes a large art filled house in Noosa Australia, a 10,000 sq. ft. office in Copenhagen and an apartment in Kensington. **Design philosophy:** dare to be different, sophisticated and sexy.

TINA GUREVICH & EKATERINA POPOVA

Designers: Tina Gurevich & Ekaterina Popova. Specialising in luxury, residential interior design. Current projects include a large apartment on the Black Sea coast, an apartment in Moscow and a villa. **Design philosophy:** eco conscious, discreet luxury.

KATHLEEN HAY

Designer: Kathleen Hay. **Company:** Kathleen Hay Designs, Nantucket, USA. A full service interior design firm specialising in residential and commercial projects that tell stories through lives well lived. Current projects include a modern home in Miami Beach, a private estate in Greenwich, CT, a seaside compound on Nantucket Island, and a restaurant in a historic building in Frankfort, Kentucky. Recent projects include a popular restaurant hotspot in Charleston, South Carolina, several summer estates on Nantucket, and a family compound in Martha's Vineyard. **Design philosophy:** filled with chic comfort.

GUOXING JIANG

Designer: Guoxing Jiang.
Company: Xupin Space Design Ltd, Kunshan, China. Covering restaurants, hotels, offices, clubs and residential. Current projects include the planning and design of a characteristic block in Guangzhou, commercial space in Xinjiang and residential space in Kunshan. Recent work includes office space in Shanghai, a restaurant in Fujian and a hotel in Suzhou.
Design philosophy: integrating Jiangnan culture into original design.

NIKKI DRUMMOND

Designer: Nikki Drummond. **Company:** Nikki Drummond Design, Cape Town, South Africa. Offering an exclusive combination of interior architectural design and interior decoration, for both residential and commercial spaces. Current projects include a home in Constantia, Cape Town, a beach house in Hermanus, Western Cape and the conversion of a magnificent manor farmhouse into a co work space and offices in Hillcrest, Durban. Recent work includes a farmhouse kitchen in Kloof, Durban, an apartment in Sea Point, Cape Town and a home in Constantia. **Design philosophy:** to create individual sensory spaces, filled with character.

VALERIYA MOSKALEVA (RAZUMOVA)

Designer: Valeriya Moskaleva (Razumova).
Company: Design studio by Valeriya Moskaleva, Moscow, Russia. Focussed on private residential. Current projects include apartments on the Spanish coast and in Moscow. Recent work includes apartments in Moscow and apartments for rent. **Design philosophy:** to balance art and architecture with the personal characteristics of each client.

CINDY RINFRET

Designer: Cindy Rinfret. **Company:** Rinfret, Ltd. Greenwich, USA. Luxury interior design and decoration in Connecticut, New York City, Palm Beach and across the United Sates, including both primary and secondary private homes for high profile and celebrity clients. Current projects include Tommy Hilfiger's newest Palm Beach home, an estate in Greenwich, CT and a new build in Palm Beach, FL. Recent work includes a historic waterfront home in Darien CT, an expansive, newly constructed residence in Wilmington, Delaware and a sophisticated Manhattan pied-à-terre for a longtime client. **Design philosophy:** comfortable yet luxurious, like the perfect cashmere sweater with jeans.

XU JINGLEI

Designer: Xu Jinglei. **Company:** Slow Coral Design, Hangzhou, China. Focusing on rural cultural tourism projects and urban boutique projects, architecture, landscape and interior design. Current work includes the industrial park of Meidu in Guangzhou, a French Michelin star restaurant in Hangzhou, and the office headquarters of Xinsheng group in Hangzhou. Recent projects include Wenzhou Valley Hotel, an art castle, Jinhaiyuan office space in Shanghai, and a health care centre in Dalian. **Design philosophy:** to create a slow, comfortable, natural and harmonious ecological circle, through traditional culture and materials for contemporary interpretation.

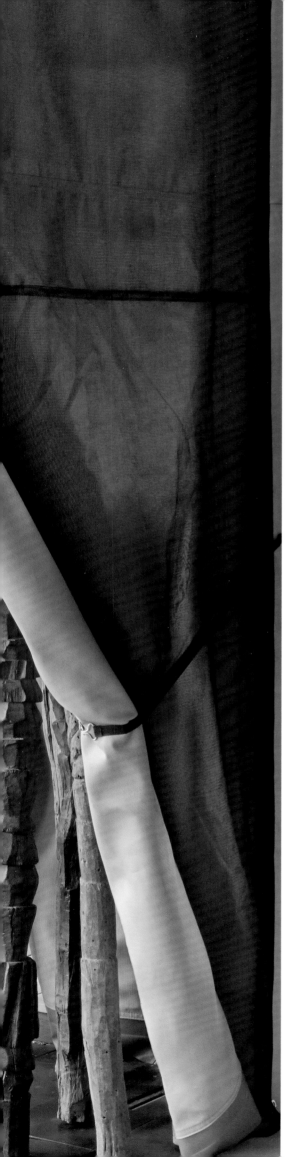

INGE MOORE & NATHAN HUTCHINS

Designers: Inge Moore and Nathan Hutchins. **Company:** Muza Lab, London, UK. Global interior designers with a diverse portfolio of projects including luxury residential developments, private homes, hotels, superyachts, restaurants & bars. Current work includes a 1930's classic yacht, a luxury residential development in Barcelona and a hotel in Milan. Recent projects include a five star resort in the Maldives, a luxury chalet in St. Moritz and a villa in St. Barts. **Design philosophy:** tactile, intuitive and contextual.

ALEXANDER KOZLOV INTERIORS

Architects: Alexander Kozlov and Anastasia Blagodarnaya. **Company:** Alexander Kozlov Interiors, Moscow, Russia. Specialising in luxury interior architecture in Russia and Europe including private homes, commercial spaces, yachts and hotels. Current projects include the renovation of 19th century mansion in Scotland, a family house in central London, an office and an apartment in a historic house in Monaco. Recent work includes an office in Moscow, a villa in France, and a spa in Moscow. **Design philosophy:** timeless.

DONNA MONDI

Designer: Donna Mondi. **Company:** Donna Mondi Interior Design, Chicago, USA. Acclaimed interior and product designer. Current work includes a modern new build home in Michigan, the interior renovation for two 1920's co ops on Chicago's East Lake Shore Drive, the interior design for a Bauhaus inspired Colorado residence, and a renovation in one of Miami's iconic buildings. Recent projects include a modern two story penthouse, an eclectic condo in Chicago's One Bennett Park high rise designed by Robert A. M. Stern Architectural Group, and six clients at the legendary No9 Walton Neoclassical luxury condo building in Chicago's Gold Coast. **Design philosophy:** Classicism x Modernity + Edge.

CHUNG-HAN TANG

Designer: Chung-Han Tang. **Company:** Design Apartment, Taipei, Taiwan. Current projects include a visitor center in Taipei, a large family home in Beijing, and executive offices in Taipei. Recent work includes a real estate sales centre in Beijing, a house in Ningbo, China, and a large family home in Taipei. **Design philosophy:** emotion expressed through materials.

ERIN MARTIN

Designer: Erin Martin. **Company:** Martin Design, St Helena, USA. 2017 designer of the year, engaged in large homes, small homes, boutique hotels, bougie hotels, quonsets. Recent projects include a 1940's Palm Springs bling house, the complete renovation of a home on The Strand in Manhattan Beach, into a Moorish, Gothic villa, and Knoll House, a new build boutique hotel nestled in a Napa vineyard. **Design philosophy:** keep going kindly.

K&H DESIGN

Designers: Katie Glaister & Henry Miller-Robinson. **Company:** K&H Design, London, UK. A six year old practice, working closely with private clients, hotel operators and developers, on new builds and listed buildings in the UK and overseas. Current projects Include the complete restoration and extension of a large semi detached Victorian house in Belsize Park, an old manor house from the Carolean period near Chichester and a classical 15,000 sq. ft. new build in Berkshire. Recent work includes the entire strip out of a rooftop apartment in Hong Kong, a five bedroom family home in Notting Hill, the entire reconfiguration of a listed duplex apartment in Eaton Square, Belgravia, entwining Brutalist interventions into the Neoclassical apartment. **Design philosophy:** meticulous and original, creating fun and beautiful homes.

DRAKE/ANDERSON

Designers: Jamie Drake & Caleb Anderson. **Company:** Drake/Anderson, NYC, USA. A multidisciplinary firm, focussed on residential and commercial projects across the globe. Current work includes a full floor apartment in the tallest residential building in the world, NYC's Central Park Tower, a Modernist ground up ski house in Deer Valley, UT, and a Neoclassical country home in Greenwich, CT. Recently completed work includes numerous apartments in Manhattan, a London townhouse in Chelsea and a Malibu estate. **Design philosophy:** sophisticated, urbane, with an element of wit.

Designers: T.K. Chu & Bryant Liu. **Company:** T.K. Chu Design, China. Specialising in luxury interior architecture in Greater China and overseas, including both primary and secondary private homes, luxury residential developments and boutique hotels. Current projects include a villa in Beijing, a residential skyscraper in Suzhou, and a seven star hotel in Shanghai. Recent work includes villas in Suzhou, a seaside apartment in Zhuhai and a sales centre in Dongguan. **Design philosophy:** Neo Art Deco, a hybrid vernacular Modernism.

T.K. CHU DESIGN

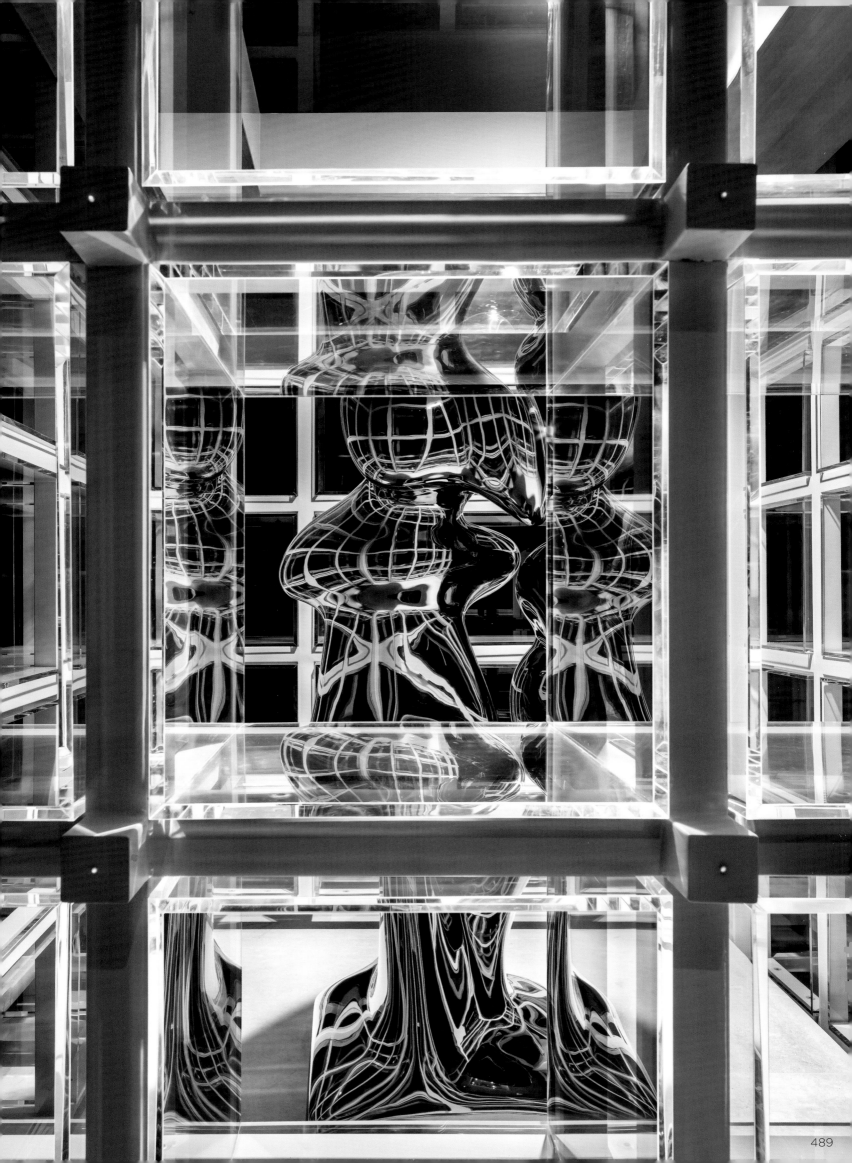

TINEKE TRIGGS

Designer: Tineke Triggs. **Company:** Artistic Designs for Living, San Francisco, USA. Award winning interior designer, specialising in high end residential projects worldwide. Recent work includes a seaside villa in Cabo San Lucas, a family beach house in Northern California, and a luxurious mountain retreat in Lake Tahoe. Current projects include a contemporary pied-à-terre in San Francisco, a modern Spanish Colonial Revival residence in Santa Barbara and a playful New England style home in Silicon Valley. **Design philosophy:** to create imaginative interiors with character and soul.

JOANNA WOOD

Designer: Joanna Wood. **Company:** Joanna Wood International Design Practice, London, UK. Joanna heads up a young, enthusiastic team experienced in creating bespoke interiors with a focus on the luxury residential market. Recent projects include the restoration of The Master's Lodge, Corpus Christi College, Cambridge, a new build house on the Dublin coast and a penthouse in Covent Garden. Current work includes the total refurbishment of a Grade II Listed house in London's oldest garden square, the conversion of a coach house in the Cotswolds and a development of nine apartments in Knightsbridge. **Design philosophy:** classical design heritage for modern living.

Designer: Jay Lee. **Company:** Mod Service Design, Shanghai, China. A well known, full cycle design service company, providing architecture, interior, furnishings, overall planning and peripheral products. Current projects include a restaurant in The Bund, Shanghai, a sales centre and model rooms in Suzhou, and a clubhouse in Nanjing. Recent work includes a sales centre and clubhouse in Zhangping, a sales centre in Hefei, and model rooms in Jiangyin. **Design philosophy:** diverse and stylish.

ALEXANDRA KIDD

Designer: Alexandra Kidd. **Company:** Alexandra Kidd Design, Sydney, Australia. A broad range of customised design solutions for residential and commercial interiors. Current projects include a cliffside coastal home, a heritage listed family home and two penthouse suites on Sydney Harbour. Recent works include an inner city Sydney pad for a New York based family, a holiday beach house and an award winning Georgian mansion in Sydney's Bellevue Hill. **Design philosophy:** 'we believe that well considered design truly can change lives.'

511

HUMBERT & POYET

Designers: Emil Humbert & Christophe Poyet.
Company: Humbert & Poyet, Monaco. Providing a full range of services from construction to interior design. Current projects include three 5 star hotels in South Korea, luxury apartments in Paris, London and Monaco, and a historic villa in Lake Como. Recent work includes Beefbar Paris, the Villa Odaya in Cannes, 26 Carré Or, a luxury 19 story residential building in Monte Carlo, and Mandarin Oriental in Vienna. **Design philosophy:** respect the soul of the site.

BRENDAN WONG

Designer: Brendan Wong. **Company:** Brendan Wong Design, Sydney, Australia. A boutique studio with a reputation for restrained luxury. Current work includes a Mt Hotham ski chalet, a Palm Beach waterfront home and a harbourside penthouse transformation. Recent projects include a Southern Highlands estate and various homes for a loyal UK and USA expat client base. **Design philosophy:** partnering a sophisticated aesthetic with uncompromising functionality to exceed client expectation.

KRIS LIN

Designer: Kris Lin. **Company:** Kris Lin International Design, Shanghai, China. Serving the top 100 real estate developers for twenty years. The business covers sales offices, clubs, art galleries, hotels, luxury villas and apartments, offices, public and commercial space. Current projects include a sales centre in Chongqing, an apartment in Shanghai, and a club house in Shaoxing. Recent work includes White Mountain Club House in Nanjing, Skylight sales centre in Yiwu, and apartment Fantasia Luwan 68 in Shanghai. **Design philosophy:** renovation comes from unique observation.

CONRAD MORSON

Designer: Conrad Morson **Company:** Conrad Alexander Design, London, UK. An upcoming design studio focusing on commercial and residential projects across the globe. Current work includes an alfresco bar and restaurant experience in the heart of Covent Garden inspired by the highly acclaimed flower market. Recent projects include a bistro bar called Mrs Riot; a character played by 18th century actress Kitty Clive who lived on the street and performed at The Royal Drury Lane Theatre. **Design philosophy:** anything is possible.

460 **Alexander Kozlov & Anastasia Blagodarnaya.**
Alexander Kozlov Interiors, Moscow, Russia.
Tel: +7 495 18 18 210
ak@alexanderkozlovinteriors.com
www.alexanderkozlovinteriors.com
(Photographer: Stephan Julliard)

508 **Alexandra Kidd.**
Alexandra Kidd Design, NSW, Australia.
Tel: +61 (02) 9331 1554
info@alexandrakidd.com
www.alexandrakidd.com
(Photographers: Justin Alexander, Brigid Arnott)

258 **Allison Paladino.**
Allison Paladino Interior Design & Collections, Palm Beach, FL, USA.
Tel: 561 814 2838
zita@apinteriors.com
www.apinteriors.com
(Photographer: Sargent Photography)

188 **ANGELOS ANGELOPOULOS ASSOCIATES DESIGN+.**
Athens, Greece.
Tel +30 210 7567191
design@angelosangelopoulos.com
www.angelosangelopoulos.com
(Photographer: Christos Drazos)

76 **Ben Wu.**
W.Design, Shanghai, China.
Tel: +86 (21) 64713899
marketing@wsdeco.com.cn
www.wdesign.hk
(Photographers: Quansheng Xiahou, PIANFANG STUDIO, Sui Sicong)

306 **Benjamin Johnston.**
Benjamin Johnston Design, Houston, Texas, USA.
Tel: +1 713 300 9203
info@benjamin-johnston.com
www.benjamin-johnston.com
(Photographers: Julie Soefer, Benjamin Johnston Design)

518 **Brendan Wong.**
Brendan Wong Design, Surry Hills, NSW, Australia.
Tel: + 612 9699 3228
info@brendanwong.com
www.brendanwong.com
(Photographer: Maree Homer)

52 **Camilla Clarke, Ottalie Stride, Ben Johnson, Anthony Kooperman.**
Albion Nord, London, UK.
Tel: +44 (0)7766250535
camilla@albion-nord.com
www.albion-nord.com
(Photographers: Brotherton Lock, Perry Graham & Patrick Williamson)

408 **Cécile Demole, Alice Cajka, Ema Salas.**
DÔME PROJECT INTERIORS, Mies, Geneva, Switzerland.
Tel: +41 22 362 74 70
　　+1 242 808 20 80
contact@dome.ch
(Photographers: Dorrie Mcveigh, Marie Cajka, Laurianne Monnier)

148 **Chang Ching-Ping.**
Tienfun Interior Planning Co. Ltd, Taiwan, China.
Tel: +886 4 22018908
tf@mail.tienfun.tw
www.tienfun.com.tw
(Photographers: Liu, Chun-Chieh, Sebastien Veronese, Chou, Yueh-Hsiang, Chen, Yao-Cheng, Chang, Ching-Ping)

236 **Charu Gandhi.**
Elicyon Ltd, London, UK.
Tel: +44 (0)203 772 0011
studio@elicyon.com
(Photographers: Patrick Williamson, Michael Sinclair)

226 **Chris Goddard.**
Goddard Design Group, Springdale, AR, USA.
Tel: +001 (479) 521 2592
chris@goddarddesigngroup.com
www.goddarddesigngroup.com
(Photographer: Mark Jackson – Chroma)

468 **Chung-Han Tang.**
Design Apartment, Taipei, Taiwan.
Tel: +886 2 23775101
da.mkt@da-interior.com
www.da-interior.com
(Photographer: One thousand degrees)

444 **Cindy Rinfret.**
Rinfret, Ltd. Interior Design & Decoration, Greenwich, CT, USA.
Tel: (1) 203 622 000
info@rinfretltd.com
www.rinfretltd.com
www.instagram.com/rinfretltd
www.facebook.com/rinfretltd
(Photographers: Neil Landino, Kimberly Garvin)

184 **Claudia Pelizzari, David Morini.**
PELIZZARI STUDIO. Milan/Brescia, Italy.
Tel: +39 030290088
studio@pelizzari.com
www.pelizzari.com
(Photographers: Giorgio Baroni, Mattia Aquila)

110 **Colette van den Thillart.**
Colette van den Thillart Interior Design, Toronto, Canada.
Tel: +1 647 964 4456
info@colettevandenthillart.com
www.colettevandenthillart.com
(Photographers: Chris Tubbs, Laura Resen, Virginia Macdonald, Melanie Acevedo, Max Kim-Bee, Nickolas Sargent)

526 **Conrad Morson.**
Conrad Alexander Design, London, UK.
Tel: +447585618844
info@conradalexanderdesign.com
www.conradalexanderdesign.com
(Photographer: Jake Davis, Instagram: jakephillipdavis)

134 **David Yu.**
Matrixing, Shanghai, China.
Tel: +86 13247641032
ypj@matrixdesign.cn
www.matrixdesign.cn
(Photographer: Shixiangwanhe)

314 **Donald Nxumalo.**
Donald Nxumalo Interiors, Sandton, South Africa.
Tel: +27 72 484 8344
info@donaldnxumalo.com
www.donaldnxumalo.com
(Photographers: Sarah Depina & Annelize Nel)

464 **Donna Mondi.**
Donna Mondi Interior Design, Chicago, Illinois, USA.
Tel: + 1 (312) 291 8431
info@donnamondi.com
www.donnamondi.com
(Photographers: Werner Straube, Paul Moore)

202 **Ekaterina Iakovenko.**
JP Interior Design, Moscow, Russia.
Tel: +79099753710
jpekaterina@gmail.com
www.jpinteriors.ru
(Photographer: Sergey Krasyuk)

318 **Elena Spiridonova & Roman Andrusenko.**
Copper&Tin, Moscow, Russia.
info@coppertin.com
www.coppertin.com
(Photographers: Mikhail Loskutov, Sergey Krasyuk)

514 **Emil Humbert & Christophe Poyet.**
Humbert & Poyet, Monaco.
Tel: +377 93 30 22 22
info@humbertpoyet.com
(Photographer: Francis Amiand)

474 **Erin Martin.**
MARTIN DESIGN, Saint Helena, Ca, USA.
Tel: 707 963 4141
info@erinmartin.com
www.erinmartin.com
(Photographer: Tubay Yabut)

218 **Frankie Fan.**
D+DESIGN OFFICE, Beijing, Shanghai, Shenzhen, Wuhan & Chengdu, China.
Tel: +86 18611167000
cd@d-design.ltd
www.d-design.ltd
(Photographers: Yunfeng Shi and Bin Jia)

248 **Gang Cao.**
Henan Erheyong Architectural Decoration Design Co. Ltd, Zhengzhou, China.
Tel: 0371 633 80939
Mobile: 1383 718 0399
13837180399@163.com
www.ehydesign.com
(Photographer: Xinwei Wang)

58 **Géraldine B. Prieur.**
ROUGE ABSOLU, Paris, France.
info@rougeabsolu.com
www.rougeabsolu.com
(Photographer: ROUGE ABSOLU)

44 **Gracinha Viterbo.**
Viterbo Interior Design, Lisbon, Portugal.
Tel: + 351 21 464 6240
Tel: + 44 20 3575 1040
info@viterbo-id.com
www.viterbointeriordesign.com
(Photographers: Francisco Nogueira, Francisco Almeida Dias)

206 **Greg Natale.**
Greg Natale Design, Sydney, Australia.
Tel: +61 2 8399 2103
info@gregnatale.com
www.gregnatale.com
(Photographer: Anson Smart)

430 **Guoxing Jiang.**
Xupin Space Design Ltd, Kunshan, China.
Tel: 0512 55215666
609927421@qq.com
www.xupin.com
(Photographer: Wu Hui)

22 **Idmen Liu.**
IDMatrix, Shenzhen, China.
Tel: +86 15986695159
ljh@matrixdesign.cn
www.ldm.com.cn
(Photographer: Shixiangwanhe)

454 **Inge Moore & Nathan Hutchins.**
Muza Lab, London, UK.
Tel: +44 207 100 3300
studio@muzalab.com
www.muzalab.com
(Photographers: Mark Williams, Brechenmacher & Baumann, Belmond)

276 **Janie Molster.**
Janie Molster Designs, Richmond, USA.
Tel: 804 282 0938
info@janiemolsterdesigns.com
www.janiemolsterdesigns.com
(Photographers: Gordon Gregory, Mali Azima)

482 **Jamie Drake & Caleb Anderson.**
Drake/Anderson, NYC, NY, USA.
Tel: 212 754 3099
info@drakeanderson.com
www.drakeanderson.com
(Photographer: Stephen Kent Johnson)

502 **Jay Lee.**
MOD Service Design, Shanghai, China.
Tel: +86 (021) 3653 8558
info@modid.com.cn
www.modid.com.cn
(Photographers: Yanming Studio, Zebra Visuals)

252 **Jeffreys Interiors.**
Edinburgh, Scotland.
Tel: +44 (0)131 247 8010
design@jeffreys-interiors.co.uk
www.jeffreys-interiors.co.uk
(Photographer: ZAC and ZAC)

212 **Jennifer Garrigues.**
Jennifer Garrigues Interior Design, Palm Beach, FL, USA.
Tel: (561) 659 7085
info@jennifergarrigues.com
www.jennifergarrigues.com
(Photographer: Tria Giovan)

418 **Jimmie Karlsson & Martin Nihlmar.**
Jimmie Martin, London, UK.
Tel: +44 (0)20 7938 1852
info@jimmiemartin.com
www.jimmiwmartin.com
(Photographer: Elayne Barre)

272 **Joana Aranha and Marta Aranha.**
Joana Aranha Studio, Lisbon, Portugal.
Tel: +351 210 960 670
info@joanaaranha.com
www.joanaaranha.com
(Photographer: Ana Paula Carvalho)

498 **Joanna Wood.**
Joanna Wood International Design Practice, London, UK.
Tel: +44 (0)207 730 0693
info@joannawood.com
www.joannawood.com
(Photographer: Astrid Templier)

198 **Joe Cheng, Ken Hu, Aiden Du.**
Cheng Chung Design (HK) Ltd., Shenzhen, China.
Tel: (86 755) 2399 6457
pr@ccd.com.hk
www.ccd.com.hk
(Photographer: Wang Ting (SensoryDesign)

338 **Jorge CAÑETE.**
INTERIOR DESIGN PHILOSOPHY, Vaud, Switzerland.
Tel: +41 78 710 25 34
info@jorgecanete.com
www.jorgecanete.com
(Photographer: Patrice Schreyer)

392 **Karen Howes.**
Taylor Howes Designs, London, UK.
Tel: +44 (0)207 349 9017
admin@taylorhowes.co.uk
www.taylorhowes.co.uk
(Photographers: Astrid Templier, Edmund Dabney)

128 **Katharine Pooley.**
Katharine Pooley Ltd, London, UK.
Tel: +44 (0)207 584 3223
enquiries@katharinepooley.com
www.katharinepooley.com
(Photographer: James McDonald)

426 **Kathleen Hay.**
Kathleen Hay Designs, Nantucket, Massachusetts, USA.
Tel: +1 508 228 1219
info@kathleenhaydesigns.com
www.kathleenhaydesigns.com
(Photographers: Joe Keller, Cassandra Michelle, Matt Kisiday)

478 **Katie Glaister & Henry Miller-Robinson.**
K&H Design, London, UK.
Tel: +44 (0)207 7363 610
studio@kandhdesign.co.uk
www.kandhdesign.co.uk
(Photographers: Simon Brown and Paul Raeside)

30 **Katie Ridder.**
Katie Ridder Inc., New York City, NY, USA.
Tel: +1 (212) 779 9080
info@katieridder.com
www.katieridder.com
(Photographers: Thomas Loof, Eric Piasecki)

158 **Kelly Hoppen CBE**
Kelly Hoppen Interiors Ltd, London, UK.
Tel: +44 (0)207 471 3350
info@kellyhoppen.co.uk
(Photographers: Sui Sicong, Tonino Lamborghini)

522 **Kris Lin.**
Kris Lin International Design, Shanghai, China.
Tel: +86 (0)21 6283 9605
krislindesign@vip.163.com
www.klid.com.cn
(Photographer: Kris Lin)

268 **Lin Xu.**
Space³ Interior Design, ShenYang, China.
Tel: +8613478893351
511160953@qq.com
www.space-interiordesign.com
(Photographer: Hongyi Mao)

232 **Li Xiang.**
X+Living, Shanghai, China.
Tel:+86 21 34613871
press@xl-muse.com
www.xxxxx.design
(Photographer: Shao Feng)

70 **Maira Koutsoudakis & Tony Pereira.**
LIFE Interiors, Johannesburg, South Africa.
Tel: +27 82 566 3138
info@life.za.com
www.life.za.com
(Photographers: Crookes and Jackson, David Crookes, Nicola Jackson, Dook, Elsa Young, Maira Koutsoudakis, Michael Poliza)

300 **Marc Hertrich & Nicolas Adnet.**
STUDIO MHNA, Paris, France.
Tel: +33 1 43 14 00 00
contact@studiomhna.com
www.studiomhna.com
(Photographers: Francis Amiand,
Studio MHNA)

334 **Mari Vattekar Markman.**
Vattekar Markman
Interiørarkitektur,
Oslo/Norway & Stockholm/Sweden.
Tel: +47 90 27 07 90 &
       46 76 763 81 61
info@vattekarmarkman.com
www.vattekarmarkman.com
(Photographer: Anne Nyblaeus)

118 **Mark Rielly, Jon Case, Michele
Rhoda.**
ARRCC, Cape Town, South Africa.
Tel: (+27) 021 468 4400
info@arrcc.com
www.arrcc.com
(Photographer: Adam Letch)

98 **Mary Douglas Drysdale.**
Drysdale Design Associates,
Washington, USA.
Tel: 1 202 588 0700
marydouglasdrysdale@yahoo.com
www.MaryDouglasDrysdale.com
(Photographers: John Cole and Ron
Blunt)

398 **Meg Lonergan.**
Meg Lonergan Interiors, Houston,
Texas, USA.
Tel: +1 713 300 2344
info@meglonergan.com
www.meglonergan.com
(Photographers: Par Bengtsson,
Stephanie Silber, Kerry Kirk, Hector
Manuel Sanchez, Megan Lovoi, Max B,
Jack Thompson)

352 **Meryl Hare.**
Hare + Klein, Sydney, Australia.
Tel: +612 9368 1234
info@hareklein.com.au
www.hareklein.com.au
(Photographer: Jen Wilding)

372 **Miaoyi Jiang & Jianhong Pan.**
**Gold Mantis Construction
Decoration Ltd,** Shanghai, China.
Tel: +86 21 62300273
30504648@qq.com
www.goldmantis.com
(Photographer: Chunfeng Zhao)

104 **Michelle Nussbaumer.**
Ceylon et Cie, Texas, USA.
Tel: 214 742 7632
info@michellenussbaumer.com
info@ceylonetcie.com
(Photographers: Douglas Friedman,
Stephen Karlisch, Melanie Acevedo)

310 **Nanjing Matilian Space Design.**
China.
Tel: 0086 173 68691537
       0086 025 52388668
1157919303@qq.com
(Photographer: ingallery)

164 **Natalia Belonogova.**
NB-Studio, Moscow, Russia.
Tel: +7 985 762 43 77
       +7 495 959 31 10
belonogova@gmail.com
nb@nb-studio.ru
www.nb-studio.ru
(Photographer: Mikhail Loskutoff)

360 **Neha & Sachin Gupta.**
Beyond Designs, New Delhi, India.
Tel: +44 (0)20 7731 6557
contact.beyonddesigns@gmail.com
www.beyonddesigns.in
(Photographer: Atul Pratap Chauhan)

262 **Nicky Dobree.**
Nicky Dobree Interior Design Ltd,
London, UK.
Tel: + 44 (0)20 7828 5989
studio@nickydobree.com
www.nickydobree.com
(Photographer: Philip Vile)

436 **Nikki Drummond.**
Nikki Drummond Design, Cape Town,
South Africa.
Tel: +27 (0)82 344 0108
nikki@nikkidrummonddesign.com
www.nikkidrummonddesign.com
(Photographer: Greg Cox)

142 **Nini Andrade Silva.**
Atelier Nini Andrade Silva, Lisbon,
Portugal.
Tel: +351 218 123 790
Mobile: +351 965 011 493
geral@niniandradesilva.com
(Photographers: Nick Bayntun,
Henrique Seruca, José Cunha)

380 **Olga Hanono Hilu.**
OLGA HANONO, Mexico City/New
York City, USA.
Tel: +5552021020
oh@olgahanono.com
www.olgahanono.com
(Photographers: Frank Lynen,
Jaime Navarro)

66 **Olga Sedova, Prokhor Mashukov.**
ONLY design, Moscow, Russia.
Tel: +7 (903) 775 70 28
o.b.sedova@gmail.com
www.only-design.com
@onlydesign_inst
(Photographer: Sergey Krasyuk,
Stylist: Natalia Onufreichuk)

172 **Patrick Sutton.**
Baltimore, MD, USA.
Tel: 410 783 1500
www.patricksutton.com
(Photographers: Richard Powers,
Stacy Zarin Goldberg)

368 **Patsy Blunt.**
Patsy Blunt Interiors, Surrey, UK.
Tel: +44 (0)1344845594
patsy@patsybluntinteriors.com
www.patsybluntinteriors.com
(Photographer: Jonathan Little)

388 **Peng Zheng.**
C&C Design Co. Ltd, Guangzhou,
China.
Tel: +86 20 89028525
c_c_ltd@126.com
www.cocopro.cn
(Photographers: Si Zifeng, Qin
Zhaoliang, Huang Zaohui)

404 **Philip Tang & Brian Ip.**
PTang Studio Ltd, Hong Kong, China.
Tel: +852 2669 1577
office@ptangstudio.com
www.ptangstudio.com
(Photographers: Hey Cheese, Ulso
Tsang, Chen Kang)

376 **Pippa Paton.**
Pippa Paton Design Ltd,
Oxfordshire, UK.
Tel: +44 1865 595470
scott@pippapatondesign.co.uk
www.pippapatondesign.co.uk
(Photographer: Paul Craig)

322 **Rebecca Buchan.**
Denton House Design Studio,
Salt Lake City, USA.
Tel: +1 801 333 8156
info@dentonhouse.com
www.dentonhouse.com
(Photographer: Sargent
Photography)

384 **Robert Kaner.**
Robert Kaner Interior Design,
New York, USA.
Tel: +1 212 727 721
info@kanerid.com
www.kanerid.com
(Photographer: Tria Giovan)

290 **Rosa May Sampaio.**
Rosa May Arquitetura de Interiores,
São Paulo, Brazil.
Tel: +55 11 3085 7100
       +55 11 99974 5251
rosamaysampaio@terra.com.br
www.rosamaysampaio.com.br
@rosamaysampaioarq
(Photographer: Alain Burgier)

296 **Ryo Aoyagi, Shuhei Kiyono, Makiko Goto, Naohiro Yoshida, Masahiro Kaihoko, Akemi Kato, Satsuki Nagashima.**
KKS GROUP (Kanko Kikaku Sekkeisha), Tokyo, Japan.
Tel: +81 3 6430 9011
contact@kkstokyo.co.jp
www.kkstokyo.co.jp
(Photographers: Mr. Koji Okumura, Forward Stroke Inc.)

242 **Sandra Lucas & Sarah Eilers.**
Lucas/Eilers Design Associates,
Houston, Texas, USA.
Tel: +1 713 784 9423
design@lucaseilers.com
www.lucaseilers.com
(Photographers: Julie Soefer, Stephen Karlisch, David Marlow)

92 **Sophie Paterson.**
Sophie Paterson Interiors, London, UK.
Tel: +44 (0)1372462529
info@sophiepatersoninteriors.com
www.sophiepatersoninteriors.com
(Photographers: Ray Main, Julian Abrams)

222 **Stefano Dorata.**
Studio Dorata, Rome, Italy.
Tel: +39 (0)68084747
studio@stefanodorata.com
www.stefanodorata.com
(Photographer: Giorgio Baroni)

88 **Stéphanie Coutas.**
GALERIE STEPHANIE COUTAS,
Paris, France.
Tel: +33 (0)1 81 29 31 90
sc@stephaniecoutas.com
www.stephaniecoutas.com
(Photographers: Francis Amiand, Gilles Trillard)

356 **Steve Leung.**
Steve Leung Design Group,
Hong Kong, China.
Tel: +852 2527 1600
comm@steveleung.com
www.sldgroup.com
(Photographer: Mr. Chen Zhong)

348 **Suzanne Lovell.**
Suzanne Lovell Inc., IL, USA.
Tel: +1 312 595 1980
contact@suzannelovellinc.com
www.suzannelovellinc.com
(Photographers: Steve Hall & Kendall McCaugherty © Hall + Merrick Photographers, Katrina Wittkamp)

8 **Thomas Jayne.**
Jayne Design Studio,
NYC, USA.
Tel: 212 838 9080
info@jaynedesignstudio.com
www.jaynedesignstudio.com
(Photographers: Don Freeman, Paul Hingham, Pieter Estersohn)

178 **Timothy Oulton & Simon Laws.**
Timothy Oulton Studio, London, UK.
Tel: +44 (0)20 3150 2024
enquiries@timothyoultonstudio.com
www.timothyoultonstudio.com
(Photographers: Graz Lam, Alex Chomicz, Jingkang Zhu, Zhaoliang Qin)

422 **Tina Gurevich & Ekaterina Popova.**
Moscow, Russia.
Tel: +7 (903) 960 3290
      +7 (925) 506 0409
tinagurevich@gmail.com
instagram.com/tinagurevich
5060409@mail.ru
instagram.com/popovadesign.ru
(Photographer: Mikhail Stepanov)

492 **Tineke Triggs.**
Artistic Designs for Living, San Francisco, California, USA.
Tel: +1 415 567 0602
info@adlsf.com
www.tineketriggs.com
(Photographers: José Manuel Alorda, Paul Dyer, Drew Kelly, Brad Knipstein, Aubrie Pick, Suzanna Scott, Christopher Stark)

488 **T.K. Chu Design.**
Taiwan, Beijing & Shanghai, China.
Tel: +86 10 85714166 813
heydenny@163.com
www.tkchudesign.com
(Photographer: Ting Wang)

344 **Tomoko Ikegai.**
ikg inc., Tokyo, Japan.
Tel: +81 3 6277 3544
info@ikg.cc
www.ikg.cc
(Photographer: Nacása & Partners Inc.)

440 **Valeriya Moskaleva (Razumova).**
Valeriya Moskaleva (Razumova) Design Studio, Moscow, Russia.
Tel: +7 926 336 4047
leraart@inbox.ru
www.m-diz.com
(Photographer: Mikhail Loskutov, Stylist: Julia Chebotar)

82 **Woodson & Rummerfield's House of Design.**
Los Angeles, CA, USA.
Tel: +1 (310) 659 3010
info@wandrdesign.com
www.wandrdesign.com
IG: Woodson_Rummerfields
(Photographers: Karyn Millet, Angela Marklew, Mary E. Nichols)

124 **Wu Licheng.**
HYMC Architectural Engineering Design Co. Ltd, Guangzhou, China.
Tel: 020 34164318
www.behance.net
(Photographer: Wu Licheng)

284 **Wu Wenli.**
Huge Rock Design, Shenzhen, China.
Tel: +8613246683650
447405560@qq.com
www.hrdsz.com
(Photographer: Chen WeiZhong)

168 **Xie Peihe.**
AD Architecture,
Shenzhen, China.
Tel: +861 599 491 5055
(Photographer: Ouyang Yun)

448 **Xu Jing Lei.**
Slow Coral Design, Hangzhou, China.
Tel: +86 0571 56770853
hzmanshanhu@163.com
(Photographer: Ye Song)

414 **Yong Wang.**
Beijing Wuxiang Space Architecture Design Studio, Beijing, China.
Tel: +010 6436 6520
wuxiang108@126.com
www.wuux.net
(Photographers: Yunfeng Shi, Yingyuyingxiang)

328 **Yuan Jiang, Chen Song.**
SODA, Beijing, China.
Tel: : +86 18610471317
office@soda.archi
www.soda.archi
(Photographer: Xiyu Chen)

364 **Young Huh.**
Young Huh Interior Design, New York, NY, USA.
Tel: 212 595 3767
info@younghuh.com
www.younghuh.com
(Photographers: Francesco Lagnese, Manuel Rodriguez, Ngoc Minh Ngo, John Bessler, John Hall, Brittany Ambridge, David Land)

14 **Zaha Hadid Architects.**
London, UK.
Tel: +44 (0)20 7253 5147
press@zaha-hadid.com
www.zaha-hadid.com
(Photographers: Scott Francis, Hufton+Crow, Paul Warchol, Luke Hayes, Virgile Simon Bertrand, Laurian Ghinitoiu, Jacopo Spilimbergo)

38 **Zhang Can, Li Wenting.**
CSD Design, Chengdu, China.
Tel: +0086 86263030
319469931@qq.com
(Photographer: Wang Ting)

© 2021 Andrew Martin International

Editor Martin Waller
Project Executive Annika Bowman
Design by Renart Design Limited

Production by Nele Jansen, teNeues Verlag
Editorial coordination by Inga Wortmann-Grützmacher, teNeues Verlag
Colour separation by Chris Chadbon Printing

Published in 2021 by teNeues Verlag GmbH

teNeues Verlag GmbH
Werner-von-Siemens-Straße 1
86159 Augsburg, Germany

Düsseldorf Office
Waldenburger Str. 13, 41564 Kaarst, Germany
e-mail: books@teneues.com

Augsburg/München Office
Werner-von-Siemens-Straße 1
86159 Augsburg, Germany
e-mail: books@teneues.com

Berlin Office
Lietzenburger Str. 53, 10719 Berlin, Germany
e-mail: books@teneues.com

Press department Stefan Becht
Phone: +49-152-2874-9508 /
+49-6321-97067-97
e-mail: sbecht@teneues.com

teNeues Publishing Company
350 Seventh Avenue, Suite 301, New York,
NY 10001, USA
Phone: +1-212-627-9090
Fax: +1-212-627-9511

www.teneues.com

ISBN 978-3-96171-369-1
Library of Congress Number: 2021935369
Printed by PB Tisk, Czech Republic

Bibliographic information published by the Deutsche Nationalbibliothek
The Deutsche Nationalbibliothek lists this publication in the Deutsche Nationalbibliografie; detailed bibliographic data are available on the Internet at dnb.dnb.de.